GOODBYE, MY FANCY

GOODBYE, MY FANCY

A COMEDY

by

Fay Kanin

SAMUEL FRENCH
25 WEST 45TH ST., NEW YORK 19
7623 SUNSET BLVD., HOLLYWOOD 46
LONDON   *TORONTO*

PRINTED IN THE UNITED STATES OF AMERICA
BY THE VAIL-BALLOU PRESS, INC., BINGHAMTON, N. Y.

For Michael

"GOODBYE, MY FANCY" was first produced by Michael Kanin in association with Aldrich and Myers at the Morosco Theatre in New York City on November 17, 1948. The play was staged by Sam Wanamaker, the scenery was designed and lighted by Donald Oenslager, and the costumes were designed by Emeline Roche. Madeleine Carroll headed the cast which was as follows:

(In order of their appearance)

GINNY MERRILL	Bethel Leslie
AMELIA	Sally Hester
CLARISSE	Gerrianne Raphael
MARY NELL	Mary Malone
MISS SHACKLEFORD	Eda Heinemann
JANITORS	Andrew George / John Ware
TELEPHONE MAN	Tom Donovan
SUSAN	Patty Pope
GRACE WOODS	Shirley Booth
AGATHA REED	Madeleine Carroll
ELLEN GRISWOLD	Lulu Mae Hubbard
PROFESSOR BIRDESHAW	Lillian Foster
CAROL	Betty Lou Holland
JO	Lenore Garland
DOCTOR PITT	George Mitchell
JAMES MERRILL	Conrad Nagel
PROFESSOR DINGLEY	Ralph Bunker
MATT COLE	Sam Wanamaker
CLAUDE GRISWOLD	Joseph Boland

The entire action of the play takes place over Commencement Weekend in early June 1948 in a dormitory room of Good Hope College for Women in Good Hope, Mass.

ACT ONE

Friday morning.

ACT TWO

Scene I: Saturday afternoon.
Scene II: Saturday evening.

ACT THREE

Sunday afternoon.

ACT ONE

ACT ONE

SCENE: *With the possible exception of twins and matrimony, there is no relationship closer both spiritually and physically than that peculiar educational phenomenon known as "room- mates." Outside the U.S.S.R., communal living has no purer form.*

If you don't believe it, take a look at the sitting room of a student suite in a dormitory of Good Hope College for Women in Good Hope, Mass. There are two of almost everything— two small desks, two reading lamps, two pin-up boards full of a heterogeneous collection of pictures, notes, memos. There's only one portable radio-victrola. But that's all right, because the other portable radio-victrola is in the bedroom, entered through a door down Left. Though you can't see it, you know the bedroom contains two beds, two dressers, two mirrors and so on ad infinitum.

Hope Hall was endowed by a rich and sentimental alumna with a love for old Gothic architecture, and so the room has the grace of a window seat bay with leaded windows and a small but nice stone fireplace. Otherwise it has the kind of simplicity dictated by college dormitory budgets.

Ordinarily, the room is very neatly kept, but today, as the Curtain rises, it's bedlam. There are several suitcases standing in the Center of the room and a couple of heavy cartons obvi- ously in the process of being filled. Some tennis rackets, a bow and a quiver of arrows, and a pair of English riding boots are spilling off a chair. One of the pin-up boards is down and lean- ing against a desk, and a stocking hanger with four dampish stockings is swinging gently from the neck of a standing lamp. At stage Left, the victrola is playing a jive record.

GINNY MERRILL *enters through the corridor doorway. She's nineteen—alert, intelligent, sensitive. She wears a cotton sun- dress and sandals, carries a book. She looks around at the state*

3

of the room with surprise. AMELIA, *an excited Senior, races in from the bedroom, carrying an armload of clothes.*

AMELIA. Oh, Ginny! Mary Nell's been trying to find you all over. [*Over her shoulder.*] Do we take any of the stuff in here?

MARY NELL'S VOICE. No. Janitors can get that. Thanks.

[AMELIA *exits as* CLARISSE, *another Senior, enters from the bedroom with her arms full.*]

CLARISSE. [*Excitedly.*] You're doubling up with us. [*She goes out.*]

GINNY. Hey! What's going on?

[MARY NELL *enters from the bedroom, carrying a pair of skis.* MARY NELL *is very pretty, even in faded jeans and run-over moccasins.*]

MARY NELL. Well, it's about time! Where've you been?

GINNY. At the Libe.

MARY NELL. At the Libe? Finals are all over.

GINNY. People sometimes go to libraries even when they're *not* cramming for exams.

MARY NELL. [*Crossing to put down the skis.*] I've got most of your stuff packed anyway.

GINNY. What's the rush? We've got another three days on campus.

MARY NELL. [*Bursting.*] Guess who's going to stay here— right in these rooms?

GINNY. [*Turning off the victrola.*] Agatha Reed?

MARY NELL. [*Disappointed.*] How did you know?

GINNY. That's what I've been doing at the Libe. Reading up on her. [*She holds up the book.*] *Women in the Vanguard.* Tells all about her college days. How she and her roommate had the two corner rooms on the first floor of Hope Hall. [*Looking out the window.*] With the windows facing the willow trees.

MARY NELL. Isn't it exciting? Imagine her looking at these same walls, studying at the same desks—

GINNY. Going to the same john.

MARY NELL. Gives me goose pimples.

GINNY. I thought she was going to stay at the Dean's.

MARY NELL. They got a wire this morning not to meet her at the station—a friend's *flying* her down instead. And she hopes they're planning to let her stay in her old rooms at Hope Hall.

GINNY. [*Suddenly noticing the empty space.*] Where's our sofa?

MARY NELL. They took it away. Someone got the idea to find the original furniture. You better start on the junk over there. We can sort it out later.

GINNY. I wonder what she's like.

MARY NELL. Busty, probably. Most women with brains, I notice it goes right to their bust.

GINNY. I don't mean what she looks like.

MARY NELL. Well, she's getting an honorary degree, isn't she?

GINNY. Oh, that's just a racket. [*As MARY NELL looks at her, shocked.*] Well, isn't it? Some celebrity gets a few fancy letters after his name. School gets publicity or a new wing on the science building. Good business.

MARY NELL. You make it sound awful, Ginny. After all, Agatha Reed is a—

GINNY. Oh, I don't mean her exactly. Matter of fact, she's one of the few who might deserve it. She's *done* something.

MARY NELL. I should think so, writing for all those newspapers. And now, being in Congress.

GINNY. Nuts. Anyone can be in Congress these days. It's what they do there that counts.

MARY NELL. I thought they just voted on things.

GINNY. Really, Mary Nell, for someone who's graduating—

[MISS SHACKLEFORD *enters from the hall, followed by two* JANITORS *carrying a faded love seat.* MISS SHACKLEFORD *is also faded, but she makes up for it with an overwhelming air of authority. She is the Alumnae Secretary, and has been as long as practically anybody can remember.*]

MISS SHACKLEFORD. Put it right over there—in front of the table. [*As they set it down.*] Carefully, now. It's not very sturdy.

MARY NELL. [*Disappointed.*] Is *that* it?

MISS SHACKLEFORD. Yes. We did the best we could with it on such short notice.

[*The* JANITORS *exit.*]

GINNY. [*Trying it.*] You mean Agatha Reed sat here? [*Wincing.*] Spring's broken.

MISS SHACKLEFORD. Well, they can't expect sentiment *and* comfort. I've just spent the whole morning tracking it down —to one of the basement rooms.

GINNY. Such is fame.

MISS SHACKLEFORD. It's very generous of you girls—giving up your rooms. But then, it's quite an honor. It'll be something to tell your children.

MARY NELL. Like people who slept in Napoleon's bed. [*Hastily.*] I mean after he was dead, of course.

MISS SHACKLEFORD. Of course. Did your father happen to mention what time her plane might be arriving, Virginia?

GINNY. [*Freezing.*] I don't see Father except on holidays, Miss Shackleford. I live here in the dorm, you know.

MISS SHACKLEFORD. Well, I just thought he might have. [*As she exits.*] Now where are those men with the rest of the things—?

GINNY. She's a finger-down-the-throat, if I ever saw one.

MARY NELL. Oh, Alumnae Secretaries have to gush around. The Alums like it. Besides, you're too sensitive about your father, Ginny. Everybody knows you don't take advantage of it. If *my* father was president of this college, I'd have lived in a penthouse on top of the Libe and never taken gym—

GINNY. Is that all?

MARY NELL. And had men imported from Princeton every weekend.

[MISS SHACKLEFORD *re-enters with the* JANITORS *who are carrying a framed reproduction, a small step-ladder and a Windsor chair.*]

MISS SHACKLEFORD. [*Giving orders.*] Over the fireplace. You can take the other one down. Put that chair there—and move the dictionary stand over there.

GINNY. Why, that's Uncle Willy!

[*She's staring at the picture one* JANITOR *is hanging.*]

MISS SHACKLEFORD. I think you're mistaken, Virginia. That's "The Laughing Cavalier" by— [*Stuck.*]

GINNY. Frans Hals. I know. But father has one just like it in his study. We always called him Uncle Willy.

MISS SHACKLEFORD. This is your father's. We borrowed it. Somebody remembered one like it used to hang in this room.

[*A* TELEPHONE MAN *enters. He's quite young, nice-looking— a fact* MARY NELL *doesn't miss.*]

TELEPHONE MAN. This where the phone extension goes?

MISS SHACKLEFORD. Yes, put it—well, wherever telephones go.

[*As the* TELEPHONE MAN *goes about wiring the extension to one of the desks,* MISS SHACKLEFORD *turns to the* JANITORS.]

You can take the rest of those things.

MARY NELL. There's still some stuff we haven't taken down—

GINNY. Let's leave a little. It'll make her feel more at home.

[*There's a moment in which everyone seems to get in everyone else's way. A box crashes to the floor.*]

MISS SHACKLEFORD. Organization, everyone! We'll never get through the weekend like this without organization.

[*The* JANITORS *exit.*]

GINNY. I'd better take a last look in the bedroom.

[*She exits into bedroom as* SUSAN, *a Junior student, enters through the hall doorway.*]

SUSAN. Miss Shackleford, there's a man outside with a tree.

MISS SHACKLEFORD. Oh yes, for the Tree Planting Ceremony.

SUSAN. He says, "Where do you want it?"

MISS SHACKLEFORD. Well, let me see—someplace near the Ivy Arch. [*Looking out the window.*] My goodness, not that monster! I distinctly told him a very young tree—practically a branch. [*Heading for the door.*] I told him we wanted to plant it ourselves. Well, he'll just have to take it right back—

[*She exits,* SUSAN *after her.*]

TELEPHONE MAN. [*Into telephone.*] Hello, Ed? It's all set.

[GINNY *enters from the bedroom.*]

MARY NELL. Find anything else?

GINNY. [*Throwing her a shower cap.*] Behind the radiator.

MARY NELL. My God! I lost it Junior Year.

TELEPHONE MAN. [*Crossing to the door.*] You can use that phone now.

MARY NELL. Thank you.

TELEPHONE MAN. Mind if I keep the telephone number?

[MARY NELL *gives him a freeze. He turns up his coat collar, exits.*]

MARY NELL. He's cute. [*Turning immediately to the telephone.*] Wouldn't it have been wonderful if we'd had it all last year? I could have talked to Sam without the whole floor listening in.

GINNY. It never seemed to inhibit you any.

MARY NELL. [*Draping herself across the window seat.*] I don't know. There's something about talking to a man when you're lying down— [*She languidly picks up the phone.*] Da-arling— Of course I love you, you silly fool. Last night? Da-arling, let's have no regrets. Until tomorrow, then—Au revoir.

[*Wearily, she drops the telephone back on its hook. It rings, suddenly. They both jump as if they've never heard a telephone before. It rings again.*]

GINNY. Well—answer it.

MARY NELL. [*Picking it up gingerly.*] Hello? Hello— What? Oh. [*Cupping her hand over the mouthpiece.*] It's long distance. New York! [*Into telephone.*] No, she isn't here yet. I said, she isn't here yet.—Who? [*Her eyes widen and she cups her hand over the mouthpiece again.*] It's *Life* Magazine! [*Into telephone.*] No. No, this is Mary Nell Dodge.—Mary Nell Do— I don't think you'd know even if you *could* hear me. —Yes, they're expecting her very soon.—Yes, I'll tell her. I'll write it down. [GINNY *notes it on a pad as* MARY NELL *says it.*] *Matt Cole.* Delayed.—Yes, I certainly will. [*She hangs up.*]

GINNY. *Life* Magazine?

MARY NELL. They're sending a man over to cover the whole weekend!

[*A woman appears in the doorway, carrying a briefcase, a portable typewriter, and one small suitcase. She's in her late forties, almost exactly* MARY NELL'S *description of a brainy woman—plenty busty. It just so happens, though, that she's not Agatha Reed but her secretary,* GRACE WOODS, *better known around Washington circles as* WOODY.]

MARY NELL. [*Recognizing her as* AGATHA.] Oh, they just hung up! Maybe you could still get the Operator.

WOODY. Who just hung up?

MARY NELL. *Life* Magazine!

WOODY. Oh.

MARY NELL. Their man got held up in New York, but he'll be here as soon as he can. [*She hands* WOODY *the paper.*] It's all written down.

WOODY. [*Taking the paper unexcitedly.*] Uh-huh.

[*She crosses to the desk, and puts down her briefcase and typewriter. The* GIRLS *stare at her, fascinated.*]

GINNY. I'm Ginny Merrill. And this is my roommate, Mary Nell Dodge.

WOODY. How are you?

GINNY. It's a great pleasure to have you here—in our rooms.

MARY NELL. We would have been out sooner. Except things got a little mixed up.

WOODY. [*Walking toward the bedroom door.*] This the bedroom?

GINNY. Yes. [*After* WOODY *exits into it.*] Doesn't she remember?

MARY NELL. It's been a long time.

GINNY. [*Bleakly.*] Anyway, you were right.

MARY NELL. About what?

GINNY. [*Pantomiming the bust profile.*] And I thought—

[MARY NELL *quiets her as* WOODY *re-enters, crosses to the desk, opens the briefcase and starts to take out some papers.*]

MARY NELL. [*Tentatively.*] I suppose you've noticed—

WOODY. What?

MARY NELL. [*Pointing to it.*] The sofa.

WOODY. Could stand recovering.

GINNY. They thought you'd like it this way.

MARY NELL. Carted it all the way up from the basement.

GINNY. [*Indicating "The Laughing Cavalier."*] And the picture—

WOODY. They cart that up from the basement, too?

GINNY. [*A little angry.*] We'd better go, Mary Nell. And leave Miss Reed alone—with her memories.

WOODY. Miss Reed *is* alone with her memories. Outside, under a tree.

MARY NELL. Then, who—?

WOODY. Me? I just carry the typewriter.

GINNY. Oh, her secretary! [*Happily.*] How do you do?

MARY NELL. She must be under the willows!

[*They dash to the window and hang out. Not much of them except two excited behinds is visible as* AGATHA REED *enters. As far from* MARY NELL'S *expectations as possible, she's undoubtedly the best thing that's happened to the United States Congress in a long time. She wears a smart lightweight suit and carries her hat and a small suitcase.*]

WOODY. [*Indicating the two behinds.*] Your reception committee.

[*The* GIRLS *turn at the voice. But* AGATHA *doesn't even notice. She's drinking in the room, her face suffused with nostalgia. She wanders around touching the sofa, fingering the desk, standing for a second under the picture of "Uncle Willy."*]

They all watch her—the GIRLS *respectfully,* WOODY *disgustedly. Finally, she disappears into the bedroom.*]

MARY NELL. Gosh! I felt like I was in church!

GINNY. Doesn't anybody know she's here?

WOODY. I doubt it. She had the taxi stop two blocks away so we could take some short cut.

MARY NELL. Through the alfalfa field—behind the gym!

WOODY. Yeah—! [*Irritably picks things off her stockings.*]

GINNY. [*Picking up the skis.*] We'd better tell them she's here. [*She exits.*]

WOODY. Give her five minutes. Let her have a good cry.

MARY NELL. We'll give her *ten* minutes.

WOODY. Five's enough. Let's not overdo it.

MARY NELL. I'm leaving her my vic. There's some Sinatras and Comos. And a keen Stan Kenton.

WOODY. Oh—peachy! [MARY NELL *hurries out.* WOODY *picks up the telephone.*] Hello. How late does Western Union stay open?—I see. What about the switchboard here? Somebody on it all night? [AGATHA *enters from the bedroom.*]—Well, could we arrange that? Miss Reed may have to be in touch with Washington at any hour. Fine. [*She hangs up.*]

AGATHA. [*Wiping her eyes.*] I haven't cried in years. It feels wonderful.

WOODY. It looks lousy.

AGATHA. You don't understand. You just see a collection of buildings, a gate, some ivy—

WOODY. What do *you* see?

AGATHA. Myself at eighteen—eager, expectant, a little frightened. Asking—what is life? What am I? This is where it all starts.

WOODY. You sound like an alumnae bulletin.

AGATHA. Don't you even believe in colleges?

WOODY. I don't believe in looking at the past. I was born in Newark, New Jersey. Every time I go through on a train, I pull down the shade.

AGATHA. You ought to see a psychoanalyst.

WOODY. I just don't get it, that's all. A crowded calendar, two important bills coming out of committee, an election just four months off—and we're braiding a daisy chain.

AGATHA. Look, Woody, let's get this settled right now. I've come down here to *enjoy* this weekend. I'm going to cry, I'm going to be silly, I'm going to be sentimental, I'm going to walk barefoot down memory lane with ivy entwined in my hair. If you don't like it, you don't have to look.

WOODY. [*Shrugs and picks up her notebook.*] What do you want to do about that Madison Square Garden rally? There's a choice of dates.

AGATHA. [*Plaintively.*] Not now—

WOODY. The world doesn't stop, even for Honorary Degrees.

AGATHA. [*With a sigh.*] All right, tell them I think it should be the earliest date they can get. [*Sitting on the sofa, she winces.*] They never fixed it!

WOODY. Fixed what?

AGATHA. The spring. Ellie broke it when she got her junior grades. She thought old Dennis was going to flunk her. When she got the C, she jumped up and down on the sofa for ten minutes.

WOODY. I'll wire them you'll speak—if they can make it next week. Who's Ellie?

AGATHA. My roommate, Ellen Thatcher. She was a beautiful girl. They called us Sugar and Spice. [*Crossing to the window seat.*] We used to sit over here—on this window seat—spring nights after Lights Out and talk about Life. [*Smiling.*] We had a pact. Wherever in the world we were, we'd send each other a telegram when we lost our respective virginities.

WOODY. Well?

AGATHA. Whatever happens to all girlhood pacts?

WOODY. [WOODY *grunts eloquently and turns over to the next sheet of paper.*] Mrs. S. Arthur Poinceford invites you for a cruise on her yacht the week of the twenty-ninth. Down to Florida—back by Monday.

AGATHA. That's the oil lobby. Tell her oil and water don't mix. [*At the desk.*] There's a little secret panel in this desk. [*She pulls out a drawer and feels around behind it.*] I used to hide brownies in it. You share your clothes, your perfume, even your themes with your roommate. But not your brownies. Not the— [*She reacts suddenly, draws out a small box, opens it.*] Brownies!

WOODY. God, they must be stale.

AGATHA. [*She tastes one. Relieved.*] Fresh this week. [*She offers the box to* WOODY.]

WOODY. [*Grimacing.*] Horrible stuff. Sticks to the roof of your mouth.

AGATHA. Now I *know* you need a psychoanalyst.

WOODY. [*Consulting the paper in her hand.*] Hope you feel photogenic. *Life's* covering the weekend.

AGATHA. Oh, that's nice.

WOODY. You *must* be getting important. They're sending Matt Cole down.

AGATHA. [*Turning abruptly.*] Who?

WOODY. Matt Cole, the war photographer.

AGATHA. You're joking.

WOODY. That's what it says here. [*Reading.*] "Matt Cole delayed." One of the kids took the message.

AGATHA. Why should they send *him* down here? This isn't his kind of thing at all. It's—it's ridiculous.

WOODY. [*Shrugging.*] Maybe he needs a vacation.

AGATHA. [*Obviously perturbed.*] You call Henry Luce. They've got twenty men that can do a better job on this sort of thing. Tell him I *don't want Matt Cole*—I'd consider it a personal favor if he'd see to it.

WOODY. Why bother?

AGATHA. [*Firmly.*] I *want* to bother.

WOODY. [*Shrugging.*] You're the boss. Might've been interesting, though. [*Picking up the telephone.*] Get me New York. —Yeah— *Life* Magazine.—All right, put it through whenever the circuits *are* free. [*She hangs up.*] The circuits are busy.

AGATHA. Well, keep after it.

GINNY. [GINNY *has appeared in the hallway. She knocks against the framework to attract their attention.*] I'm sorry to disturb you—

AGATHA. Oh, that's all right—

GINNY. But I forgot something. [*She starts toward the desk.*]

AGATHA. I'm afraid I found them. I've been a pig about it, too.

[*She holds the box of brownies toward* GINNY.]

GINNY. Oh, you keep them.

AGATHA. You won't have to twist my arm. I don't get brownies very often. Not good ones like these.

GINNY. I made them myself.

AGATHA. Really? What do you use—whole chocolate or ground?

GINNY. Chocolate *syrup*. That's the secret. It's what makes them so wet.

WOODY. Oh, brother! [*She crosses to the bedroom and exits.*]

GINNY. [*Going to the desk.*] I didn't really come for the brownies. I always hide the book I'm reading in here. It's the only way I can get to finish it without somebody waltzing in and borrowing it. [*She fishes a book out of the secret panel.*]

AGATHA. Is it good, the book?

GINNY. It's *Leaves of Grass* by Walt Whitman.

AGATHA. Oh, I'm very fond of Walt Whitman.

GINNY. [*Pleased.*] Are you?

AGATHA. Matter of fact, I have a favorite.

GINNY. Which one?

AGATHA. It's a rather obscure one. "Goodbye, my fancy, Farewell, dear mate, dear love. I'm going away, I know not where—"

GINNY. "—Or to what fortune, or whether I may ever see you again. So goodbye, my fancy." [*They look at each other in mutual appreciation.*] I like that one, too. I'd never read much Whitman till Dr. Pitt gave me the book.

AGATHA. Your English teacher?

GINNY. No, Physics.

AGATHA. Oh. [*Smiling.*] Walt Whitman seems a little far afield.

GINNY. You don't know Dr. Pitt. When he teaches, you learn about everything.

AGATHA. Sounds as if I'd like to know him. [*Examining GINNY.*] Do you want to be a poet?

GINNY. Oh, no.

AGATHA. What *do* you want to be?

GINNY. I don't know yet. I guess that sounds odd from a college Senior. Only—I think it's more important to know what you want than what you want to be. Does that make sense?

AGATHA. [*Impressed.*] Yes, of course. [*Then.*] You know, I don't know your name.

GINNY. I'm sorry. It's Ginny. Ginny Merrill.

AGATHA. How do you do? [*They shake hands.*]

GINNY. Mary Nell's telling them you're here. I'd better be going. I guess they'll all be in soon.

AGATHA. Sounds very formal. Better comb my hair. [*She starts toward the bedroom, suddenly stops herself.*] Merrill. [*Turning.*] Your parents—will they be here for Commencement?

GINNY. There's just my father.

AGATHA. Oh. Does he—have to come very far?

GINNY. [*Uncomfortably.*] No. As a matter of fact—

AGATHA. You're Jim Merrill's daughter!

GINNY. Yes.

AGATHA. I should have known.

GINNY. Why?

AGATHA. You look like him. Something you do with your mouth when you talk— [*Feeling it suddenly necessary to explain.*] I knew your father very well. He was *my* favorite professor.

GINNY. I always forget Father once taught History 101A. [*Then.*] What was he like?

AGATHA. Very handsome. All the girls were in love with him.

GINNY. They still are. Old as he is.

AGATHA. Not so old.

GINNY. In his forties.

AGATHA. [*Amused.*] I guess it depends on your point of view.

GINNY. Was he a good teacher?

AGATHA. Very. He had a way of making history come to life. Not just dates and battles but real things that happened to real people. I remember once I cried all night when he told us about John Brown. It was the most wonderful thing that happened to me my whole Freshman year.

GINNY. Did he know about it?

AGATHA. Yes. I wrote him a note and told him. And he wrote me back a note. I remember what it said. [*Smiling.*] "My dear Miss Reed— I'm sorry I made you cry. I shall try to make up for it next month when we discuss the Coolidge administration."

GINNY. [*After a moment.*] I wish he was still a teacher.

AGATHA. Why? Is being President of the College so bad?

GINNY. It's—different.

AGATHA. A little heavier on the dignity side, I guess.

GINNY. Yes.

[*A woman appears in the doorway. She has the look of a beauty who has eaten too many finger sandwiches at too many afternoon teas. She wears an expensive print dress and a much-too-fancy hat, and carries a large paper hat box. This, I'm sorry to say, is* ELLEN GRISWOLD, *née Thatcher.*]

AGATHA. [*Seeing her.*] Ellie—!

ELLEN. Ag—! [*They come together and embrace in a very genuine rush of emotion.*] It's so good to see you. I heard you'd arrived and I had to hurry over before the others.

GINNY. [*Rising.*] I'd better be going.

ELLEN. Oh, hello, Ginny.

GINNY. Hello, Mrs. Griswold.

AGATHA. [*Crossing to* GINNY.] Wait a minute. I'll be seeing you again, won't I?

GINNY. Oh yes. Matter of fact, I'm supposed to be getting dressed right now to be introduced to you.

AGATHA. Well, let's call this a rehearsal.

[GINNY *smiles and exits.* AGATHA *turns to* ELLEN *who's looking up at the picture of "Uncle Willy."*]

ELLEN. Uncle Willy doesn't look a day older, does he?

AGATHA. Wasn't it nice of them to remember? [*Noticing the box* ELLEN's *carrying.*] What's all that?

ELLEN. Just some old things I've saved. I dug them out when I heard you were coming. [*She takes them out of the box one by one and hands them to* AGATHA.] That sketch I made of Smitty in art class. You put the mustache on it, with real hair. Remember? [*As* AGATHA *nods, she takes out a stuffed doll with red wool hair.*] Clara Bow. You forgot to take her when you left. [*Another piece of paper.*] The theme you wrote for me when I had the hangover from Dartmouth Winter Carnival. [*She takes out a victrola record.*] And one of our old victrola records. Betty Boop. Our favorite. [*She sees the victrola and, crossing, puts the record on the turntable.*] Let's hear it again.

AGATHA. [*Stopping her.*] Later, later— [*Holding her off.*] I haven't had a chance to look at you.

ELLEN. [*Defensively.*] I've put on some weight, I know. Too many bridge luncheons. And Claude won't let me diet.

AGATHA. Claude. That's your husband.

ELLEN. Yes.

AGATHA. [*Trying to remember.*] I never met him, did I?

ELLEN. No, I didn't meet him myself till a few years after I'd left school. We had one of those big church weddings— I sent you an invitation.

AGATHA. I was in Spain. I found it when I got back.

ELLEN. Claude and I nearly went to Spain on our honeymoon. [*Searching.*] There was some reason—

AGATHA. The war.

ELLEN. [*Vaguely.*] War—?

AGATHA. The Spanish Civil War. That was my first big newspaper job.

ELLEN. Oh, that's right. That's the one where the Russians were fighting it out with the Nazis or something.

AGATHA. Well, not quite.

ELLEN. Oh, it's all too much for me. I don't bother with those things. If there's anything I want to know I just ask Claude. [*As* AGATHA *looks at her.*] It's convenient having a husband.

AGATHA. So I've been told.

ELLEN. [*With a touch of embarrassment.*] You know, I never did send you that telegram—like we promised. I guess I figured the wedding invitation would—

AGATHA. It did.

ELLEN. [*Archly.*] I've never gotten one from you either.

AGATHA. Must have slipped my mind at the moment. [*As* ELLEN'S *back straightens ever so slightly, she changes the subject.*] I hear you have a child.

ELLEN. *Two.* Both boys. I'd like to have a girl but it's so much trouble at my age. Maybe you can come to dinner and see them. We have a big barn of a house—eighteen rooms. I could have just a few people, the Mayor and the Falkners—that's Falkner Tools. And most of the trustees are in town. Claude's Chairman of the Board of Trustees, you know.

AGATHA. No, I didn't.

ELLEN. Ever since the year I was elected President of the Alumnae Association. It's so cute—the interest he takes in the school. Gets a big kick out of it when the girls call him Daddy Griswold. He's always giving them things. This year it's a projection booth and movie equipment. They're renaming the theatre—*Griswold* Theatre.

AGATHA. Oh yes, Miss Shackleford wrote and asked me to bring down a documentary film from Washington—for the program this weekend. So I brought my own.

ELLEN. Your own?

AGATHA. Yes. *Fight to the Finish.* It's based on a speech of mine.

ELLEN. Isn't that wonderful? You know, I always talk about how I knew you when. How we all voted you the-girl-most-likely-to-succeed. [*A pause.*] Of course, I never say anything about your being expelled.

AGATHA. Thank you. [*Amused.*] I guess there won't be much said about that this weekend.

ELLEN. I never did understand it, Agatha. Student Court was so hush-hush about it, nobody could find out a thing. Of course, everyone knew there was a man connected with it. You don't get expelled for staying out all night unless there's a man connected with it.

AGATHA. [*Staring at her.*] You know, I've got the most peculiar feeling, Ellen. That you haven't changed—at all.

ELLEN. Thank you! That's what Claude says. He says if I ever change he'll divorce— [*Suddenly reacting to something she sees out the window.*] Here they come—the whole delegation! [*To* AGATHA, *reproachfully.*] You upset the applecart, you know. They had an elaborate welcome planned for you at the railroad station.

AGATHA. Oh, I'm sorry.

ELLEN. [*Peering through the window.*] Miss Shackleford, leading the way, and the Student Committee. Miss Birdeshaw—you remember her—?

AGATHA. Old Fun-in-Bed Birdeshaw?

ELLEN. Still here. And still teaching Physiology. Only now they call it Sex Hygiene. [*Squinting.*] And a man— [*Surprised.*] Why, it's Dr. Pitt. Isn't it just like Shackleford to pull a boner and put him on the Reception Committee?

AGATHA. Dr. Pitt? Physics professor?

ELLEN. Yes.

AGATHA. Why, a boner?

ELLEN. Well, Claude says he's a troublemaker. Jim's going to get rid of him next year. [*Then.*] You knew they made Jim Merrill President, the year after you left?

AGATHA. Yes, I read it in the papers.

ELLEN. It was quite an honor—he was pretty young for it. And generally they bring in a President from outside. But he was so terribly popular, And he's done a great job. [*She straightens her hat.*] I'm glad I came ahead, Agatha. I wanted this cozy little chat with you alone, just like old times. I've enjoyed it.

AGATHA. I have too, Ellen. [*Wryly.*] It's the first time in years I've been alone with anyone that I haven't been asked what's going on in Washington.

ELLEN. Oh, you never have to worry about that from me. I always say the less women worry about the government, the better. [*Realizing it's a faux pas.*] Except *Congresswomen,* of course.

[AGATHA *is looking at her, almost as if she can't believe it, as the whole delegation enters the room. The* GIRLS *are in white dresses—each carries a bouquet of flowers.* MISS SHACKLE-

FORD, *in the vanguard, sweeps up to* AGATHA *and shakes her hand.*]

MISS SHACKLEFORD. [*Resoundingly.*] Welcome home, Agatha Reed!

AGATHA. Thank you, Miss Shackleford.

MISS SHACKLEFORD. Or should I call you—the Honorable?

AGATHA. Definitely not.

MISS SHACKLEFORD. [*Chidingly.*] I see Mrs. Griswold's been the early bird. But I'm sure she's been telling you how honored Good Hope is to welcome back one of its *favorite* graduates.

AGATHA. Not *quite* a graduate.

MISS SHACKLEFORD. [*Thrown for a moment.*] Well—practically. [*Turning quickly to the rest who have grouped themselves inside the door.*] You remember Miss Birdeshaw?

[MISS BIRDESHAW *flutters forward.*]

AGATHA. Of course. [*As* MISS BIRDESHAW *shakes her hand.*] How could I forget Miss Birdeshaw? She taught me the facts of life.

MISS BIRDESHAW. [*Embarrassed.*] I never really thought of it that way.

AGATHA. You look wonderful, Miss Birdeshaw.

MISS BIRDESHAW. So do you, Agatha. Of course, a bit older— I mean, a woman instead of a—

MISS SHACKLEFORD. [*Hastily.*] Miss Birdeshaw means you look so *young* to be in Congress.

AGATHA. Maybe Congress was equally deceived, Miss Birdeshaw. At least for the first few months.

DR. PITT. September fourteenth, to be exact, wasn't it? [AGATHA *turns to look at him in surprise.*] Your atom-bomb speech on the House floor.

MISS SHACKLEFORD. [*Delighted at the coup.*] I don't believe you know Dr. Pitt, Agatha. Our Physics professor. He came to us a little after your time.

AGATHA. How do you do, Dr. Pitt? [*They shake hands.* DR. PITT *is around fifty—tall, a little drawn. There is the look about him of a man who knows a great deal, so much that there is no necessity to be constantly proving it.*] It's very gratifying, your knowing my speech. Sometimes you get a feeling on the floor of Congress, something like being on the radio—you're not quite sure anyone's listening.

DR. PITT. I know what you mean. Get somewhat the same feeling in my classroom.

[*There is a general laugh at this, especially from the Student Committee.* MISS SHACKLEFORD *beckons them forward. The* GIRLS *are eager and excited.*]

MISS SHACKLEFORD. And this is your "honor guard"—chosen to represent the activities of the college this weekend. [*Beckoning the first one forward.*] Carol Friedman—President of Student Government.

CAROL. [CAROL *steps forward, clearing her throat nervously.*] Student Government wishes to present you this bouquet, Miss Reed, as a token of their respect for one who has so well demonstrated the principle that Women can take their rightful place beside Men in the Government of this Great Nation. [*She hands* AGATHA *the bouquet and shakes hands with her.*]

AGATHA. Thank you.

MISS SHACKLEFORD. Jo Wintner—Physical Education.

JO. [JO *steps forward. She is a sturdy girl with a gruff voice.*] Phys Ed welcomes Agatha Reed, who has the spirit of Good Sportsmanship and Fair Play in all that she does.

[JO *shakes* AGATHA'S *hand in a grip that makes her wince. She hands her some flowers.*]

AGATHA. That's very sweet.

[*During this last,* WOODY *has come out of the bedroom to see what all the commotion is about. She leans against the doorframe enjoying* AGATHA'S *increasing discomfiture.*]

MISS SHACKLEFORD. Mary Nell Dodge—May Queen.

MARY NELL. [*Stepping forward.*] These flowers are for you, Miss Reed, who combines the qualities that make for True Beauty and— [*She's suddenly stuck.*]

MISS SHACKLEFORD. [*Prompting.*] Wom—

MARY NELL. [*Gratefully.*] —Womanhood Glorified! [*She hands* AGATHA *a bunch of roses and shakes her hand.*]

AGATHA. [AGATHA *avoids* WOODY's *eyes.*] Really, I—

MISS SHACKLEFORD. [*Indomitable.*] Clarisse Carter—Dramatics Club.

CLARISSE. [CLARISSE *steps forward dramatically. Her voice is a combination of Bernhardt and Duse.*] In the Theatre of Life, you have made Woman's Role more important and more truly rich. We of the Dramatic Club—applaud you, Agatha Reed!

[*She hands* AGATHA *a bouquet.* WOODY *applauds. They* ALL *turn and stare at her.* AGATHA *gives her a stern look. She stops.*]

MISS SHACKLEFORD. And last—Virginia Merrill, representing the graduating Seniors.

GINNY. [GINNY *steps forward.*] The Seniors have asked me to thank you for coming to our Commencement, Miss Reed, because your presence here gives us courage and reassurance when we need it most.

[*She and* AGATHA *exchange a warm smile as she shakes* AGATHA's *hand and hands her the flowers.*]

AGATHA. Thank you. [*To* ALL.] I'm not sure I deserve all the extremely nice things you've said about me—but I'm not going to let you take back a single one of them. [*There's an apprecia-*

tive laugh from the group.] I've thought a great deal about Good Hope in the past few years. Because of a growing feeling that the "good hope" of our world lies in the young and, most importantly, in the places where they're taught to think. Standing under the willows beside Hope Hall, and now, here in these rooms with all of you, I feel that more strongly than ever. And a fine, warm feeling of coming—home.

[*At the end of* AGATHA'S *speech,* DR. MERRILL *appears and stops in the doorway.* JAMES MERRILL *is a handsome man with the combination of virility and charm that can survive the difficult atmosphere of a girls' college. The dignity of the Presidency is undeniably on his shoulders, but there is a sense of humor with it that rescues it from pedantry.*]

MISS SHACKLEFORD. [*Crossing to him excitedly.*] Oh, Dr. Merrill! You missed our little ceremony. Miss Reed has just given our girls a very inspiring speech.

MERRILL. Yes, I heard the end of it from the hall. [*Crossing to* AGATHA.] We're very pleased to have you back, Miss Reed.

AGATHA. Thank you, Dr. Merrill.

[*She attempts to shake his outstretched hand but in the effort some of the bouquets tumble to the floor.* MERRILL *tries to help recover them—it's an awkward moment.*]

WOODY. I'll take them. [*She relieves* AGATHA *of all the flowers.*]

AGATHA. [*Gratefully.*] Thank you, Woody. [*Generally.*] My secretary, Miss Woods. [*There is an exchange of how-do-you-do's.*]

MISS SHACKLEFORD. [*Taking charge.*] Now I hate to break this up, but I'm afraid we'd better all run along. We've a very full day ahead.

[*She herds her brood toward the door and* AGATHA *crosses to shake hands and say goodbye.* DR. PITT *is the last.*]

AGATHA. Thank you so much for coming today, Dr. Pitt.

DR. PITT. I've enjoyed it, Miss Reed. [*He looks pointedly at* MERRILL.] I never expected to be put on your Reception Committee. It was a "pleasant surprise." [*To* MISS SHACKLEFORD.] Thank you, Miss Shackleford. [*He exits.*]

[*There is a strained moment.*]

ELLEN. [*Bristling.*] Well, that certainly was uncalled-for! Now I see what Claude means—

MERRILL. [*Politely but firmly.*] They tell me the Alumnae Luncheon's a sellout, Ellen.

ELLEN. Oh, yes. I'd better go and check my guest lists. I've lost part of the class of '24. See you at the speaker's table, Ag.

AGATHA. Fine.

[ELLEN *exits.*]

MISS SHACKLEFORD. Oh, Agatha. I hope you haven't forgotten that movie your promised us.

AGATHA. Didn't the print get here?

MISS SHACKLEFORD. Print?

AGATHA. Of the film. We sent it out a few days ago.

MISS SHACKLEFORD. Sent it? Oh, dear. I thought you'd *bring* it. What does it look like?

WOODY. It's round—in a tin can.

MISS SHACKLEFORD. Like sardines?

MERRILL. [*Controlling a smile.*] Maybe they delivered it right to the theatre, Miss Shackleford.

MISS SHACKLEFORD. [*Distraught.*] I'd better go down and see.

[*She hurries out.*]

AGATHA. You'd better go along, Woody. She might not recognize it.

WOODY. Recognize it? She probably *ate* it. [*She exits.*]

AGATHA. [*Apologetically.*] You mustn't mind Woody. Her mind's always on the tip of her tongue.

MERRILL. It's refreshing.

AGATHA. I stole her from a Senator who stole her from a Cabinet Member. She knows more about Washington than the FBI.

[*There is a silence for a moment, a rather awkward one. As if these two people are very aware that they are alone in a room together.*]

MERRILL. You're looking very well, Agatha.

AGATHA. Thank you, Jim. I'm tired. This session of Congress has been a little exhausting.

MERRILL. I'm afraid you're not in for much of a rest this weekend. Miss Shackleford seems to have outdone even herself.

AGATHA. Yes, I've seen the agenda.

MERRILL. I can turn my back if you'd still like to escape.

AGATHA. [*Shaking her head.*] Vanity, I guess. Secretly everyone dreams of coming back to his college for an honorary degree. It's a popular ambition—like wanting a mink coat.

MERRILL. Or to be President.

AGATHA. Yes. [*Then.*] How does it feel?

MERRILL. What?

AGATHA. To be—President.

MERRILL. [*Smiling.*] It's never dull—the faces change too often. And with so much youth around, you actually get the feeling you're preserving your own.

AGATHA. Your daughter has you "tottering" on the brink of senility. [*As he reacts.*] We had a talk. She's a lovely child. No,

that's wrong. She's not a child. What are we at that age, Jim?
At that wonderful, terrible in-between time? You've seen so
many of us.

MERRILL. Wait a minute. Now you *are* dating me.

AGATHA. Even with most of the student body in love with you?
[*As he looks surprised.*] Ginny's my authority.

MERRILL. Well, I serve a function. They sigh wistfully over
my grayed temples—until it's time to trot off to proms and
have some fun. Then they come back and sigh some more. It
gives their lives an interesting dimension.

AGATHA. There must be more to this business of being college
President than that.

MERRILL. Not much. A few good Latin phrases and one slightly
risqué story for Alumnae dinners. *Very* slightly, you understand. And, of course, a cap and gown in fairly-good condition.

AGATHA. That's an accurate description of some college Presi-
dents I know. I won't accept it for you.

MERRILL. No?

AGATHA. [*Shaking her head.*] I have a pretty vivid recollection
of your contempt for educators with banquet-side manners.
What was it you called them—Educaterers? [*She laughs. He's
looking at her oddly.*] You seem surprised I remember so well
what you said.

MERRILL. I am. You've heard a lot of people say a lot of things.

AGATHA. Yes. [*Then, quietly.*] Only you were the first. The
first who ever said anything that mattered. [*She meets his eyes
for a moment, then walks to the window.*] Do they still skate
on Horner's Pond—in the winter?

MERRILL. Yes. We've got a lodge now, with a stove for hot
coffee.

AGATHA. That sounds nice. [*After a moment.*] Once I found a little pond just like it, near a university outside Leningrad. I even wrote a piece about it. I called it—

MERRILL. Horner's Pond, U.S.S.R. [*As she turns, surprised.*] You were syndicated, you know.

AGATHA. Odd, though. That you should have read *that* one.

MERRILL. I read them all. [*She looks at him.*] Spain, China, Poland, Russia—Washington.

AGATHA. Isn't that Miss Shackleford's job—keeping track of the alumnae?

MERRILL. Sometimes she's careless.

AGATHA. [*With an attempt at casualness.*] Well, it's a good thing. Now I don't have to catch you up on all I've been doing the past twenty years.

MERRILL. No. [*Then.*] Except the first one. I've never quite— caught up on the first one. [AGATHA *reaches for a cigarette. Her hand is not quite steady.*] You don't mind my being curious?

AGATHA. No, I don't mind.

MERRILL. Maybe it's *my* vanity. But all these years I've wondered—what happened. Why you just—disappeared.

AGATHA. It was very stupid of me to get caught climbing in my window at six A.M. [*Smiling.*] I trust this generation is more adroit.

MERRILL. [*Turning away.*] I'm not up on the statistics.

AGATHA. Obviously I'm not saying this very well.

MERRILL. I shouldn't have brought it up.

AGATHA. [*Earnestly.*] It would have made no difference to the trustees that you were the man and that we were planning to be married. I would have been kicked out just the same, only you would have been kicked out with me. Not many young professors would have been so willing to give up a chance to be President.

MERRILL. We'd decided to take that chance.

AGATHA. I know. [*Simply.*] But I couldn't let you, Jim.

MERRILL. Where did you go?

AGATHA. My mother had to get over the humiliation of having a daughter expelled. I stayed with an aunt in Detroit. She'd been an old suffragette and there wasn't anything could humiliate her.

MERRILL. My letters came back. When I phoned your home, they said they didn't know where you were.

AGATHA. I made them promise that.

MERRILL. It all sounds so—

AGATHA. Cold-blooded? [*Shaking her head.*] It wasn't. At eighteen, it's very difficult to be cold-blooded. Once, I almost wrote you a letter. [*She takes a deep draw on her cigarette.*] I didn't finish it. A little later I read about your marriage in the newspaper.

MERRILL. [*After a moment.*] Did Ginny tell you anything about her mother?

AGATHA. No.

MERRILL. I'd like to.

AGATHA. It's not necessary, Jim. I didn't mean—

MERRILL. [*Firmly.*] I'd like to. [*She nods, turning away from him.*] I met her at Columbia. I'd gone down there for the summer. She was a little older than I was—but we had a lot of things in common. They helped to balance the things we— didn't have. She—well, she died when Ginny was born.

AGATHA. Why did you feel you had to tell me that?

MERRILL. I don't know exactly.

AGATHA. [*Turning to him.*] What are you trying to say, Jim?

MERRILL. You came down here this weekend. [*Searching her face.*] Why?

AGATHA. Have you forgotten? You invited me.

MERRILL. That invitation—I carried it around two years before I sent it. [*A pause.*] I thought about it five years before that.

AGATHA. That was silly. I answered it five minutes after I got it.

[*He stares at her. As if he can't quite believe it. Then, almost simultaneously, they start toward each other.* WOODY *enters. They stop in their tracks.*]

WOODY. The weekend is saved. We found the film.

[*There's a pause.* AGATHA *and* MERRILL *turn away from each other with elaborate casualness.*]

AGATHA. Oh—fine.

WOODY. [WOODY *looks from one to the other.*] I've got orders to tell you the Alumnae look hungry.

AGATHA. [*To* MERRILL.] Creamed chicken and peas?

MERRILL. You learn to accept the inevitable.

AGATHA. [*Crossing toward the bedroom.*] I'd better fix my face.

MERRILL. [*Coming up to her.*] Miss Reed, did I tell you—it's wonderful to have you back?

AGATHA. Yes, Dr. Merrill. But it's good to hear it again.

[*They smile at each other. Then* MERRILL *turns and starts to the door.*]

MERRILL. It's wonderful to have you, too, Miss Woods.

[*He exits.* WOODY, *looking after him curiously, crosses to the door and closes it. There is a silence.*]

WOODY. Nice looking—

AGATHA. Who?

WOODY. Prexy.

AGATHA. [AGATHA *is fixing her hair at the mirror.*] Yes, isn't he?

WOODY. Looked mighty cozy in here when I came in.

AGATHA. Mmm.

WOODY. Talking over old History exams?

AGATHA. [*Laughing.*] You know what's wrong with you? You're spoiled. You're so used to having your thumb in every Washington pie you can't stand missing—

WOODY. Stop filibustering.

AGATHA. All right. [*She sits down deliberately.*] It's so.

WOODY. What's so?

AGATHA. Just what you're thinking.

WOODY. Oh. [*Then.*] Well, I guess you've got to do something to give this weekend a lift. Has he got a friend for tonight?

AGATHA. [*Laughing.*] You're warm, darling. But not warm enough.

WOODY. Wait a minute! Let me get this straight—

AGATHA. It's quite simple. He was the first man I ever loved. Maybe the only one. [*As* WOODY *stares at her.*] Don't look so shocked. I'm going to marry him.

WOODY. *Marry* him?

AGATHA. He hasn't asked me yet. But he will—tonight.

WOODY. [*Hopefully.*] You're kidding.

AGATHA. Why? Are you against marriage, too?

WOODY. Good God, Agatha, I'm not against marriage. But there's a time and place for everything. [*Then.*] You're smack in the middle of an election campaign—a *hundred* things. Your life's too busy.

AGATHA. There's quite a difference between a busy life and a full one.

WOODY. [*Shaking her head.*] That's funny—coming from you. Do you know what you are to millions of American women? The embodiment of an ideal. The woman they think they'd like to be. Not just reading about history, but helping to shape it.

AGATHA. Am I all that? Sounds wonderful.

WOODY. [*Belligerently.*] It *is* wonderful!

AGATHA. You've missed the point, Woody. I don't want to be any less. I'm greedy. I want to be more.

WOODY. And he's the man to do it?

AGATHA. Yes.

WOODY. For God's sake, Agatha, when I was fourteen, *I* fell in love with the fellow who sold peanuts on our block. I'm not going to marry him.

AGATHA. Maybe you should. Maybe you have a deep and consuming need for peanuts. [*There is a silence.* AGATHA *turns away.*] I'm a little—disappointed. I hoped you'd be happy for me.

WOODY. What did you expect? I don't even *know* the guy.

AGATHA. Well, *I* know him. [*Earnestly.*] Woody, this isn't a whim. It's something I've waited for—thought about for twenty years. It may be the most important thing in my whole life. That's why I don't want anything to spoil it. I don't— [*She stops suddenly.*] What about that telephone call?

WOODY. Telephone—?

AGATHA. To *Life*. Henry Luce. About Matt Cole.

WOODY. I told you. The circuits were busy. They said they'd call me back.

AGATHA. [AGATHA *crosses abruptly to the telephone and picks it up. Into telephone.*] Hello— What happened on that call to New York? *Life* Magazine.

WOODY. What's the rush?

AGATHA. [*Into telephone.*] Oh good. Then put it right through.

WOODY. I told you I'd take care of it.

AGATHA. When? When we get back to Washington?

WOODY. I didn't know it was life and death.

AGATHA. [*Into telephone.*] Hello, is Mr. Henry Luce in?— Will you tell him it's Agatha Reed? It's very important.—Yes, I'll wait.

SUSAN. [SUSAN *comes rushing in, excitedly.*] Oh, Miss Reed! Mr. Cole just came and he's taking pictures of everybody! He wants one of you—with the graduating class!

[AGATHA'S *hand with the telephone in it drops slowly to her side. She sits down in the desk chair. The squeak of a voice is heard through the telephone. It seems to be saying "Hello" over and over.* WOODY *crosses and takes the telephone from* AGATHA.]

WOODY. [*Into telephone.*] Hello. Mr. Luce?—You'll be delighted to know. We're renewing our subscription.

CURTAIN

ACT TWO

ACT TWO

Scene I

Scene: *It is late afternoon of the following day. Some of the flowers of the day before are arranged tastefully around the room, giving the place a kind of festive air. The last afternoon sun is slanting through the windows.*

The room is empty. Through the open corridor door can be heard dimly the sound of voices and the tinkle of glass. This is Agatha's "tea" going on in the Lounge of Hope Hall. After a moment AGATHA *and two* MERRY LARKS *enter. The* MERRY LARKS *wear maroon flannel blazers with large yellow notes appliqued on them. They're talking excitedly.*

FIRST MERRY LARK. —And we tried to look for Dr. Merrill.

SECOND MERRY LARK. But then Professor Dingley came along and he said he'd take care of her—

AGATHA. I think he brought her in here. [*A rather elderly man enters from the bedroom. This is* PROFESSOR DINGLEY *who teaches Botany, and looks it.*] Oh there you are, Professor Dingley. Is Miss Birdeshaw all right?

DINGLEY. I don't know. She's resting on the bed. She looks quite pale.

AGATHA. I'm sure it's nothing serious.

DINGLEY. I've sent the janitor to bring my car around. So we can take her home.

AGATHA. Good.

DINGLEY. [*Heading for the door.*] I hope he remembers to bring it to the service entrance— [*He exits.*]

FIRST MERRY LARK. It was all so sudden. All of us Merry Larks

39

were lined up in the hall, just starting in to the lounge to sere-nade you—

SECOND MERRY LARK. And Miss Birdeshaw came along and in-sisted on singing with us—

FIRST MERRY LARK. And we didn't know what to do. Then—she just sort of—collapsed!

AGATHA. Well, don't worry about it. She probably forgot to eat lunch. [WOODY *enters from the bedroom, a wet towel in her hand.*] Now you run along and reassure the rest of the Merry Larks. [*They exit.* AGATHA *turns to* WOODY.] Poor little Birdeshaw. I'm afraid she never had a cocktail before.

WOODY. [*Mopping her own brow with the towel.*] *A* cocktail? After the second one, she started on doubles.

AGATHA. How is she?

WOODY. Stinking!

AGATHA. Oh well, I'm glad. She might've gone on all her life quietly drinking tea and died one day without ever knowing what she'd missed.

WOODY. She's missed a lot more than that. [*Then.*] What the devil does she teach around here anyway?

AGATHA. Sex Hygiene.

WOODY. Oh—no!

DINGLEY. [*Entering and crossing to the bedroom.*] It's here.

AGATHA. Fine.

[*He exits into bedroom.*]

WOODY. Did you see the way she was snuggling up to that—butterfly chaser?

AGATHA. Professor Dingley is a *botanist.* [*Smiling reminis-cently.*] She's had what was known as a crush on him since way back when I was here. We used to make jokes about how she could never even say hello to him without blushing.

WOODY. That ole debbil rum! I think she's going to hate herself in the morning.

AGATHA. [*As* PROFESSOR DINGLEY *enters carrying the prostrate form of* MISS BIRDESHAW.] Don't you need some help?

DINGLEY. No, thank you. I'll just take her home and— [*He stops, suddenly realizing what he's saying.*] Well, perhaps, it would be better if— [*He's embarrassed.*]

WOODY. Okay. You put her *on* the bed. I'll be along in a few minutes and put her *in* it.

DINGLEY. Thank you. [*He shifts the dead weight a little to get a better grip and manages to make it out the door.*]

AGATHA. [*Enjoying it.*] You're a regella Florence Nightingale.

WOODY. You know, nobody but you could get away with this. Turning a tea into a cocktail party.

AGATHA. Well, it's one of those things you promise yourself to do before you die.

WOODY. There's a lot you're getting away with this weekend. [*Chidingly.*] Keeping Prexy out till three in the morning. You know, that isn't done.

AGATHA. It's all right, Woody. You're now speaking to the future Mrs. James Merrill.

[*There is a pause.*]

WOODY. It's all—set?

AGATHA. All set.

[*There is a moment while* WOODY *struggles with her own feelings.* AGATHA *watches her expectantly.*]

WOODY. Agatha, I've been with you a long time. You always knew what you wanted. If this is it—congratulations.

AGATHA. [*Warmly.*] Thank you, Woody. Nothing's going to be different. Just better.

WOODY. You mean—I get a raise? [AGATHA *laughs.*] When's the great day?

AGATHA. Oh, we haven't talked about that yet. Matter of fact, we're going to keep it all pretty quiet until after this whole Commencement business is over.

WOODY. [*Looking out the window.*] What was all that fuss about Matt Cole? He's out there—doing his job, taking pictures like crazy.

AGATHA. Yes. I'm afraid I exaggerated that whole thing. Forget it. [MERRILL *appears in the doorway.*] Oh—Jim.

MERRILL. They told me Miss Birdeshaw had an "accident."

AGATHA. Just a little too much picnic lemonade.

MERRILL. [*Smiling.*] That's what I figured. [*Then.*] Did anyone notice?

AGATHA. I don't think so. If you have to pass out, you should do it like Miss Birdeshaw—quietly and in the hall.

[WOODY *is studying* MERRILL *with great interest.*]

MERRILL. It's a good thing the *Life* man wasn't around. [*Then.*] He told me you worked together in China.

AGATHA. Yes.

MERRILL. Is he discreet?

AGATHA. [*Shaking her head.*] I'm afraid not, but don't worry. He specializes in major indiscretions. I don't think he'll make anything of it.

MERRILL. Oh yes—he wants a picture of you, Miss Woods. Said you'd been dodging him.

WOODY. I hate *Life* photographers. They're always trying to catch you picking your nose. [*She exits pointedly closing the door.*]

[MERRILL *and* AGATHA *stand looking at each other.*]

AGATHA. You can lock the door, if you want to.

MERRILL. It's against dormitory rules. [*He crosses the room and catches her in his arms.*] And so is this. [*He kisses her.*]

AGATHA. I hate dormitory rules.

MERRILL. So do I.

AGATHA. Who makes them anyway?

MERRILL. I do. [AGATHA *laughs.*] I can't believe it.

AGATHA. What?

MERRILL. That you're here. That everything's the same. You won't run away again?

AGATHA. Not a chance. Never on second proposals.

MERRILL. Incidentally—how did they compare?

AGATHA. Well, the first one was a bit more colorful. It had one lovely quotation from Shelley.

MERRILL. Shelley! I don't believe it!

AGATHA. Would you like me to quote?

MERRILL. No! Women have such frighteningly-long memories.

AGATHA. *Some* women—for the words of *some* men. Have you any idea how many times I remembered things you said?

MERRILL. No—

AGATHA. That's how I got into politics. [*As he looks at her questioningly.*] I have a little farm in Pennsylvania where I go whenever things get too complicated. Some women change their hairstyle or take an ocean voyage. I put up chow-chow. In jars. With labels. [*Suddenly.*] Do you *like* chow-chow?

MERRILL. Very much.

AGATHA. [*Relieved.*] It's lucky. We have four hundred jars. Anyway, I was up there when a local delegation called on me. They wanted to run me for Congress—with an assist from Mr. Roosevelt. There wasn't any machine, or much money, but there seemed to be a lot of plain people who wanted to go out and ring doorbells for me. [*She pauses, remembering.*] It was all very flattering—but I didn't want to run for Congress. I just wanted to relax and get some sleep for a while. Only all that night I kept remembering something you'd once said when there was first talk of their offering you the Presidency. You were a teacher, you said, and you wanted to teach. I asked you if that meant you'd turn it down, and you said, of course not. You said that "not to go forward was to go back. That no man could afford the luxury of standing still, no matter how comfortable it was." [*A pause.*] Do you remember?

MERRILL. Yes.

AGATHA. I called them up the next morning and told them they had a candidate.

MERRILL. [*Quietly.*] That's quite a responsibility. I'm not sure I would have wanted it. [*He rises.*] I think we'd better get back in there.

AGATHA. Maybe *everybody's* passed out by now.

MERRILL. I wouldn't count on it. I'm sure Miss Shackleford hasn't passed out.

AGATHA. Or Claude Griswold.

MERRILL. What do you think of Claude?

AGATHA. He's a charm-boy, all right.

MERRILL. Well, he has his faults. But he's pleasant—and he's really interested in the school. Oddly enough, he's a great admirer of yours.

AGATHA. Oddly enough is right. My voting record can't exactly have endeared me to him.

MERRILL. [*Laughs.*] No, but he seems to like you in spite of it. [*Then.*] Maybe I'll go on ahead. It'll look less— [*He searches for the correct word.*]

AGATHA. [*Kissing him.*] Is that what you mean?

MERRILL. That's what I mean.

[*There is a knock on the door.* MERRILL *releases her quickly.*]

AGATHA. Yes?

GINNY'S VOICE. It's Ginny, Miss Reed. Are you busy?

MERRILL. [MERRILL *reacts to this information nervously. He gets out his handkerchief and dabs at his lips.*] I'd rather we didn't mention anything about this to Ginny at the moment. I'd like to tell her later—in my own way.

AGATHA. Of course, Jim. Just as you like. [*Crossing to the door, she opens it.*] Come in, Ginny.

GINNY. [*Urgently.*] Oh, Miss Reed, I'd like to ask a favor of— [*She stops as* AGATHA *indicates her father, turns and sees him.*] Oh. I didn't know you were with someone.

[AGATHA *looks from father to daughter, aware of a kind of tension.*]

MERRILL. Nothing wrong out there, is there?

GINNY. No. I—I just wanted to tell Miss Reed something.

MERRILL. [*Starting to the door.*] Well, I can take a hint. [*Noticing.*] You look very lovely today, Ginny. Is that a new dress?

GINNY. I got it last year—for Dean's Tea.

MERRILL. Oh. Didn't the flowers go well with it?

GINNY. No, the color was wrong. Maybe I can wear them to-night. Thank you for sending them. [*She stands there, tense.*]

MERRILL. Well— [*He exits.*]

GINNY. [GINNY *shuts the door. Talking fast.*] Miss Reed, there isn't much time. I told Dr. Pitt you wanted to see him. He'll be in any minute.

AGATHA. Dr. Pitt? I don't—

GINNY. I hope you don't mind. I did it without asking you— but I had to get him away. Claude Griswold's in there, sounding off all about "the next war" and Dr. Pitt's getting mad. His hands are beginning to shake like the last time. That was at Sophomore Reception and he'd been drinking that time, too.

AGATHA. [*Smiling.*] Wait a minute. I'm sure Dr. Pitt can manage a cocktail or two without—

GINNY. It's more than a cocktail or two. [*As* AGATHA *reacts.*] Oh, don't get the wrong idea. It's just lately. Since they've been trying to get him out of here. It's so unfair. He's what all teachers should be.

AGATHA. I'm sure your father appreciates that. [GINNY *withdraws.*] Why don't you tell him how you feel about Dr. Pitt? [GINNY *doesn't answer. There's a knock on the door.*]

GINNY. [*Desperately.*] You *will* pretend you asked to see him, won't you, Miss Reed? I wouldn't want him to know I— [*She stops.*]

AGATHA. Yes. Of course. [*She calls.*] Come in.

[GINNY *hurries to the desk, picks up the Walt Whitman book as* DR. PITT *enters. He looks at her, then* AGATHA.]

DR. PITT. Ginny said you wanted to see me.

AGATHA. Yes.

GINNY. [*Elaborately.*] You're quite sure you're finished with the book, Miss Reed?

AGATHA. Oh—yes.

GINNY. Well, then, I'll just take it along with me.

[*She walks past* DR. PITT, *smiles hesitantly, exits. There's a moment.*]

DR. PITT. I have a feeling I'm being saved.

AGATHA. [*Smiling.*] Well, I did want a chance to talk to you again before the weekend was over.

DR. PITT. Why?

AGATHA. Because you told me my speech was wonderful, of course. And because I have great respect for good teachers. Physics professors who give their students Walt Whitman to read.

[PITT *bows, a bit ironically. He loses his balance imperceptibly and grabs the back of a chair for support.*]

AGATHA. [*Gently.*] Would you like to sit down, Dr. Pitt? [*He smiles and sits.*] You know, I've always been curious. About what makes someone become a teacher.

DR. PITT. So have I. What do *you* think?

AGATHA. Well, it can't be the pay. It must be that one day you decide the mind of a person is the most exciting thing in the world.

DR. PITT. Isn't that a little romantic?

AGATHA. [*Laughing.*] Maybe. But I think all of us who believe in the future have to be a little "romantic."

DR. PITT. Future? I thought that word had become obsolete.

AGATHA. [AGATHA *stops smiling and looks at him for a moment.*] Ginny tells me there's some question of your staying on here. She seems to feel it's important that you do.

DR. PITT. Ginny's a nice girl. She has the eager, intense convictions of youth.

AGATHA. Isn't it good? That there's so much of it around?

DR. PITT. Not very. Not when you can't get to it.

AGATHA. You're a teacher. If anyone can get to it, you can.

DR. PITT. Can I? [*He smiles as if at a child.*] I teach Physics, Miss Reed. Only sometimes I don't. Sometimes I talk about other things. The daily headlines—the atom bomb—the world. You see, I have the dangerous misconception that the object of education is to teach the young to think. That's dangerous, because they might get to like it. [*He sits, lost for a moment, staring.*]

AGATHA. [*Gently.*] You were making a point, Dr. Pitt.

DR. PITT. Oh, yes—the point. The point is that I now teach Physics—and I stay safely within the covers of the textbook.

AGATHA. Why?

DR. PITT. Why? Because I've been given an ultimatum. I either do—or I resign. [*He smiles again.*] Oh, I thought of it. I even wrote a letter to a friend of mine at the head of the Science Department of a Texas University. He once offered me a job. The letter came back with a polite note from the Dean. My friend had "resigned" two weeks before.

AGATHA. [*Quietly.*] That can't be the end of the story, Dr. Pitt. Or you wouldn't be challenging Mr. Griswold at tea parties.

DR. PITT. [*Rising.*] Don't worry, I'm working on it. By next year, I'll be able to listen to him and not even hear.

AGATHA. And in two years you might even be agreeing with him?

DR. PITT. [DR. PITT *turns and looks squarely at* AGATHA.] I'm forty-five years old, Miss Reed! For twenty-two of those years I've fought every way I knew against ignorance, against indifference. Because I believe that people really wanted to learn. [*The anger drains out of him.*] Now I say to hell with them. If they don't care enough about it, why should I? Let their daughters bring their knitting to classes and read movie maga-

zines inside their notebook covers. Let them all be wiped off
the face of the earth without even knowing why. Like the pigs
and the mice at Bikini. Maybe it's better to die stupid, like an
animal.

AGATHA. [*Quietly.*] Dr. Pitt, I respect your fears. I'm frightened myself. Anyone who isn't frightened today is a fool. But
I never get angry at the fools. Just at the wise men, who see
the danger and run away.

DR. PITT. What would you have me do?

AGATHA. [*Encouragingly.*] First of all, stop feeling sorry for
yourself. We all know there are men who're afraid to let education have a mind and voice. But you're in a better position
than at most colleges. You can get the support of your President—and then make a real fight of it.

DR. PITT. [*After a pause.*] Merrill?

AGATHA. Yes.

DR. PITT. [DR. PITT *crosses to the window and looks out.*] Have
you seen our library, that monument to learning? And the
shiny gymnasium? Our eminent President gave up battles for
buildings a long time ago. [*He notices the look on* AGATHA'S
face.] You don't believe me?

AGATHA. No.

DR. PITT. Why? It can't be a surprise to you that a man who
gets position gets comfortable and careful. It's a fine old tradition.

AGATHA. I know Jim Merrill.

DR. PITT. Do you?

AGATHA. Yes!

DR. PITT. [*Shrugging.*] Then there's nothing to say.

AGATHA. [*Coldly.*] I'm beginning to realize I also know you,
Dr. Pitt. The weary liberal, the defeatist. I know why you

can't go to Jim Merrill. Because the weakness is in *you*—not him!

MISS SHACKLEFORD. [*The corridor door suddenly burst open under the vigorous hand of* MISS SHACKLEFORD. *Booming.*] —and this is the room where it all started. We've tried to restore the original— [*She sees* AGATHA *and* DR. PITT.] Oh, I had no idea anyone was in here.

[MATT COLE *has appeared in the doorway behind* MISS SHACKLEFORD. *He's in his forties, a large man with an easy body and a hard head. He wears a Leica camera in a case and an extra lens case over his shoulder. When he uses the camera later, it becomes part of his body, like a third hand.*]

COLE. We can come back later.

AGATHA. No, come ahead, Cole. Dr. Pitt and I were just finishing.

DR. PITT. [*A tired man.*] If you'll excuse me— [*He starts toward the door.*]

AGATHA. Dr. Pitt— [*As he turns.*] You'll probably be looking for your drink.

[*With quiet irony, she hands him the glass he's left on the table. He looks at her, then takes it silently and exits.*]

MISS SHACKLEFORD. Mr. Cole thought it would be nice to get some pictures of your room. It's such a coincidence—you and he being old friends.

AGATHA. Yes. We've run into each other all over the world.

MISS SHACKLEFORD. Photography is such a fascinating profession. Several of our girls have taken it up. Perhaps you've run across them—Mary Jessup, she was Class of '32? And Phyllis —no, it was *Evelyn* Tate, Class of '40?

COLE. Must've missed them.

MISS SHACKLEFORD. Oh well, I think they both had babies and

gave it up. [*Coyly.*] Mr. Cole, I know you have things all figured out, but I was wondering if I could make *one little* suggestion?

COLE. Sure. Go ahead.

MISS SHACKLEFORD. Well, I was thinking it would be a darling idea to do a picture of Miss Reed and Mrs. Griswold in this room with the two girls who live here now. You know, past and present?

COLE. [*To* AGATHA.] How do you feel about being—past?

MISS SHACKLEFORD. [*Hastily.*] Oh, I didn't mean that *literally.*

AGATHA. It's quite all right, Miss Shackleford. Can you get the other three rounded up?

MISS SHACKLEFORD. [*Delightedly.*] I'm sure they're all right in the lounge. [*Heading for the door.*] It won't take a minute.

[*She exits.*]

COLE. [COLE *is wandering around the room.*] So this is the cocoon.

AGATHA. I've never exactly thought of myself as a butterfly. [*He picks up the record on the victrola.*] Make yourself at home.

COLE. Thank you. [*Reading.*] Betty Boop. A memento?

AGATHA. Yes.

COLE. Touching. [*He replaces the record and snaps a quick picture of the victrola.*]

AGATHA. Have you been getting anything decent?

COLE. All *very* decent. Will you sit on the sofa, please?

AGATHA. [*As she crosses and sits.*] How did you come to get on this assignment anyway? Isn't it a little out of your line?

COLE. I asked for it.

AGATHA. Why?

COLE. Thought it might be interesting to see Agatha Reed and how she grew. [*He's wandering around her, getting an angle.*]

AGATHA. Is it?

COLE. Very. It's such a paradox.

[*She looks at him.* COLE *gets the shot.*]

AGATHA. Why paradox?

COLE. Because I don't get *you* coming out of this.

AGATHA. [*Riled.*] You've been on war fronts so long, an atmosphere like this is bound to seem a little incongruous.

COLE. Dated is the word. A kind of old-world feeling you used to connect with Europe in the twenties. The graceful yet desperate attempt to maintain the status quo.

AGATHA. Generalities are so easy.

COLE. All right, then I'll be specific. I got a shot yesterday of some of the girls here—how old are they, nineteen, twenty? [*As she nods.*] They were rolling hoops down the lawn. An old tradition. Very cute. I've got a picture I took in Rome five weeks ago. A couple of fourteen-year-old girls, soliciting on the streets. I'd like to print them side by side. Higher Education—1948.

AGATHA. Why don't you?

COLE. It's another set for Cole's Gallery. All the pictures not fit to print.

AGATHA. You must have quite a collection by now.

COLE. Enough for a book—this winter.

AGATHA. Cole, that's wonderful.

COLE. I'll send you an autographed copy. [*He sits on the arm of the sofa.*] I never got a chance to ask you—did you ever get that stuff I sent you from China?

AGATHA. Oh yes. I—[*She doesn't look at him.*]—I was so glad to have the pictures of Lao San and the kids. And the school-house. I'm sorry. I didn't know where to write to thank you.

COLE. I went on to Cairo. [*After a moment.*] Did you like the one of yourself?

AGATHA. I'm not sure. The one place you don't expect to be photographed is in bed—asleep.

COLE. Why not? It's the best time. Nothing false. No attitudes.

AGATHA. [AGATHA *gets up and crosses away from him.*] I wasn't thinking as a photographer.

COLE. Neither was I. [*She turns and looks at him quickly.*]

AGATHA. The occasion wasn't exactly the kind of thing I wanted recorded for posterity.

COLE. No? I thought it had the makings of one of the big moments of history. As I remember, you did, too.

AGATHA. War has a way of making little moments seem big at the time.

[*There is a pause.* COLE *just stares at her.*]

COLE. [*Quietly.*] Can I quote you on that, Miss Reed?

AGATHA. I'm sorry. I didn't mean that quite the way it sounded. [*Then.*] But it's true, isn't it, Cole? It's what I tried to say that day in Paris—but didn't. That it was a nice snapshot, but never a family portrait.

COLE. Such subtle distinctions escape me.

AGATHA. Oh, I'm sure you didn't come down here to dig all that up. [*Brightly.*] Come on—what'll you take for the negative?

COLE. I'll give it to you. Tied up with a pink bow. For a wedding present.

AGATHA. [*Startled.*] What kind of talk is that?

COLE. There's an overpowering odor of orange blossoms in the air.

AGATHA. How on earth?— [*Getting it.*] You took pictures of Woody just now—

COLE. She's not a bad subject. Once you pin her down.

AGATHA. [*Angrily.*] How could she?

COLE. She didn't. Just gave me a hint. Now you've confirmed it.

AGATHA. Cole, if you breathe a word of this in that article—

COLE. Don't worry. It's purely for my personal files. [*Then.*] He must be quite a guy to keep a woman like you on the hook for twenty years.

AGATHA. How did you know I—

COLE. He told me. What a brilliant History student you were.

AGATHA. You haven't wasted a minute, have you?

COLE. [*Shaking his head.*] Mmm—no.

AGATHA. [*Confidently.*] Yes, he *is*. Quite a guy.

COLE. Or else you must be getting tired.

AGATHA. What does that mean?

COLE. This overwhelming desire to return to the womb.

AGATHA. You're revolting!

COLE. Girlhood memories. Old pictures, old sofas, old records —pardon me if I throw up.

AGATHA. [*Icily.*] Have you finished?

COLE. Who're you kidding? [*Crossing to her.*] You can't bury yourself in a graveyard like this. Or on a corpse like Merrill. Anyone can see he's got no blood. They've sucked him dry.

AGATHA. Will you get out of here!

COLE. Sure. But here's another memento. Since you've gone in for collecting them.

[*He pulls her to him and kisses her. She pushes away from him.*]

AGATHA. [*Furious.*] You can't take it, can you, Cole? That he could be more exciting, more desirable than you?

COLE. That's right. I'm vain as hell.

AGATHA. Let's get this straight. You were sent up here to take pictures. Anything else is none of your damned business!

[*The door bursts open.*]

MISS SHACKLEFORD. [*Gaily.*] Here we come, ready or not! [*There's no answer.* MISS SHACKLEFORD *doesn't even notice. She has* ELLEN, GINNY *and* MARY NELL *in tow.*] Does everyone know everyone?

COLE. [*To* AGATHA'S *back, with a smile.*] All friends.

ELLEN. Miss Shackleford didn't even give me a chance to comb my hair. How does it look, Ag?

AGATHA. [*Automatically.*] Fine.

ELLEN. It's your fault if it doesn't. I'm just a wee bit tipsy. [*Reproachfully.*] Cocktails at a school tea. Of course, Claude made it clear to Mr. Cole we don't do this sort of thing all the time. He's going to make a point of that in the story, aren't you, Mr. Cole?

COLE. Yes, indeed.

MARY NELL. [*Crossing to him.*] I'm awfully excited, Mr. Cole. I never thought I'd get my picture in *Life*.

COLE. Just stick around long enough and *Life's* bound to catch up with you.

MISS SHACKLEFORD. [*Busy planning.*] Now let me see—don't you think one of Ellen and Agatha here on the sofa?

COLE. I think we can do better than that. [*To* AGATHA.] Can you suggest a "representative" pose of your student days, Miss Reed?

AGATHA. [*Icily.*] I wouldn't remember.

COLE. Maybe Mrs. Griswold could help us out.

ELLEN. Well, Ag always loved to lie on her stomach on the floor, with a pillow under her—

AGATHA. [*Hastily.*] Something in a chair near the desk would do.

COLE. Inspired. [*As* AGATHA *complies.*] And Mrs. Griswold— leaning on the desk, I think, talking. Just talking easily.

ELLEN. [ELLEN *crosses and leans stiffly against the desk.*] Now you'll tell me when, won't you, Mr. Cole? I always have to be told when.

COLE. Sure. But you can just relax now. It'll be a minute till I get the camera set. [*He sights.*]

ELLEN. [*Slumping comfortably.*] Claude has one of those expensive cameras with all the gadgets, but he never gets anything in focus. And I just pick up my little box Brownie and push the button and out come—

COLE. [COLE *takes his shot.*] Thank you.

ELLEN. [*Horrified.*] You didn't take it, did you?

COLE. Afraid I did.

ELLEN. [*Almost in tears.*] But you didn't say when. I wasn't even trying to look nice.

COLE. I have a theory about women, Mrs. Griswold. [*He looks at* AGATHA.] I think they look nicest when they're not trying.

AGATHA. [*Arising abruptly.*] Are you finished?

COLE. I think so. [*Turning to* GINNY *and* MARY NELL.] Now let's have 1948. [*As they come forward.*] I think in the same positions. Leaning against the desk, Miss—

MARY NELL. [*Selling it.*] Dodge.

COLE. [*With an appreciative appraisal of* MARY NELL.] Dodge. [*Then.*] And in Miss Reed's place, the other young lady.

MISS SHACKLEFORD. Ginny is the daughter of our President, you know.

COLE. No, I didn't. [*He looks at her with interest.*]

GINNY. [*Uncomfortably.*] I'd rather Mr. Cole didn't mention that, Miss Shackleford. If you don't mind.

[AGATHA *gives* GINNY *a disturbed glance which* COLE *doesn't miss.*]

COLE. Whatever you say. [*Sighting through his camera.*] Oh, I meant to ask you, Mrs. Griswold. Did your husband ever get hold of Dr. Merrill?

ELLEN. I think so. [*To* AGATHA.] Claude was a little worried about the movie you brought down, Agatha. Mr. Cole was telling him something about it.

[AGATHA *looks quickly at* COLE. *He smiles.*]

COLE. Woody said you were showing *Fight to the Finish* here tomorrow.

AGATHA. Yes.

COLE. I was telling Mr. Griswold it's one of the few pictures I ever saw that had real guts. Wished I'd made it myself.

AGATHA. [*To* ELLEN.] Why should Claude be worried?

ELLEN. Something about wanting to be sure it was right for our girls to see. I don't know— I never get those things straight.

MARY NELL. [*Eagerly.*] Is it censorable?

MISS SHACKLEFORD. [*Now she's worried.*] Oh, dear!

ELLEN. Well, don't everybody worry about it. Claude's taking it up with Jim now.

COLE. [*Clicking.*] That's it. [*The* GIRLS *get up.* GINNY *looks in* AGATHA's *direction apprehensively.*] I'm sorry. I hope I haven't started any trouble.

AGATHA. Not at all, Mr. Cole. I'm sure Dr. Merrill is quite capable of handling the situation.

COLE. Good. [*Unloading his camera.*] Otherwise I'd have this on my conscience.

[MERRILL *appears in the doorway.*]

MISS SHACKLEFORD. [*Dolorously.*] Oh, Dr. Merrill. I hope there isn't any trouble.

MERRILL. Trouble?

MISS SHACKLEFORD. About the movie.

MERRILL. Oh. [*His eyes go immediately to* AGATHA.]

AGATHA. [*Smiling steadily.*] Ellen tells us Mr. Griswold was concerned about it.

MERRILL. A little.

AGATHA. [*Confidently.*] I trust you reassured him.

MERRILL. Well, I had to admit I didn't know too much about it myself.

[*There is an awkward pause.*]

COLE. Shall we get on to those other pictures you suggested, Miss Shackleford?

MISS SHACKLEFORD. What other—? [*She gets it.*] Oh yes. Those *other* pictures. Come along, girls.

ELLEN. [*Taking the cue.*] Claude'll be looking for me.

[*As they all exit,* COLE *pauses in the doorway for one significant glance back at* AGATHA *and* MERRILL. *Then he goes out, closing the door. There is a little silence.*]

MERRILL. Darling, I'm very sorry this happened. I forgot to ask you anything about the picture and when it came up, I didn't really know what to say.

AGATHA. You don't think I'd have brought down anything unsuitable?

MERRILL. Of course not.

AGATHA. You know how I feel about what another war would mean. That's what this movie is—some newsreel film, illustrating a speech I once made. I even narrated it myself.

MERRILL. Agatha, I'm not questioning it at all. It's just that— all the trustees are in town. Your springing the cocktail party this afternoon got their feathers a little ruffled. So Claude feels we ought to take a look at the picture. There's just time enough to run it now. [*She's quiet.*] Darling, don't get upset. It's a shame Mr. Cole brought this whole matter up. But we'll straighten it out. [*She's still quiet.*] Look, you come with me. We'll both—

AGATHA. No. I'd rather not. I'm just a little tired.

MERRILL. Of course. You must be. I won't even see the picture. [*At her questioning look.*] Something must be wrong with my eyes. I can't seem to see anything but you. [*She smiles. He leans down and kisses her tenderly and reassuringly.*] You haven't forgotten. There's a step-sing before the Prom. I'll pick you up.

[*She nods and he exits. She stands there for a moment, then turns—her face unsmiling and troubled. Then she starts back across the room, automatically removing her earrings, unfastening her dress. As she does, her eye falls on the victrola. She stares at it, slowly lifts the hand and starts it. The voice of Betty Boop bounces out. It sounds pathetically and irretrievably dated, like the era it represents. Suddenly,* AGATHA *is afraid to listen any more. She stops the record and shuts the victrola lid as*

THE CURTAIN FALLS

ACT TWO

SCENE II

SCENE: *It is two hours later.*
The room is the same, except that all the lamps are now on, and some candles are lit on the mantel. The windows are open and lights from the building across the quad are twinkling in the summer night. The corridor door is open and through it the noise of the dormitory can be heard—a radio remotely playing a popular tune, occasional voices.
WOODY *is seated at the desk downstage, typing briskly, wearing a formal dress and her working glasses. In a second,* SUSAN *appears in the corridor doorway carrying two corsage boxes. As she starts to look in,* CLARISSE *intercepts her in the hall.* CLARISSE *is in an evening slip and stocking feet.*

CLARISSE. Hey Susie, do you remember who I loaned my gold shoes to?

SUSAN. No.

CLARISSE. Dammit, I can't find them. [*She disappears on down the hall.*]

[SUSAN *enters the room as* WOODY *continues typing. She coughs, but gets no response. Finally, she knocks on the door frame.*]

WOODY. [*Stopping the typing.*] Yeah?

SUSAN. These just came for you and Miss Reed. [*She hands* WOODY *the boxes.*] Flowers.

WOODY. Thanks. [*She puts one down, and opens hers.*]

SUSAN. [*Chattily.*] Orchestra just arrived. Twenty-two men. Last year they only had eighteen.

WOODY. Inflation.

60

SUSAN. Well, if Miss Reed needs anything, I'll be on the switch-board all night.

WOODY. Fine.

SUSAN. [SUSAN *starts to go out, then stops.*] Oh—that call you're expecting from Washington—?

WOODY. [*Expectantly.*] Yeah?

SUSAN. It hasn't come yet.

WOODY. [*Looking at her sourly.*] Oh. [*Then.*] It'll come. Look, even if I'm at this—what is it—?

SUSAN. Step-sing?

WOODY. Now wait a minute, don't tell me. They *sing*—on the *steps?*

SUSAN. Yes.

WOODY. That's what I thought. Anyway, you come out there and get me. It's important.

[*There's the remote sound of a buzzer off-stage.*]

SUSAN. There goes the board now— [*She dashes out.*]

[*Alone,* WOODY *sets her orchid down while she examines the card dangling from Agatha's box. Unfortunately, it's in a sealed envelope. She's holding it up to the light when* COLE *appears outside the window. He leans on the window sill, watching* WOODY *with interest.*]

COLE. Uh—uh—uh!

WOODY. [WOODY *jumps guiltily, sets the box down. Turning, she sees* COLE.] Oh—it's you.

COLE. Why don't you try a little steam?

WOODY. I forgot my tea kettle.

COLE. Where's the Honorable?

WOODY. In the "date room"—being interviewed by the local press.

COLE. [*As he swings his leg over the sill and sits on it.*] Too bad. Thought I might pick up a little cheesecake for the piece. How a Congresswoman dresses for a Senior Prom. Does she put her shoes on *before* her girdle or *after?*

WOODY. She doesn't wear a girdle.

COLE. The rubber lobby won't like that.

WOODY. [*Sharply.*] That's not for publication.

COLE. Who, me—?

WOODY. Don't give me those baby blues. You're about as innocent as a rattlesnake.

COLE. What'd I do now?

WOODY. I haven't forgiven you yet for spilling that marriage business.

COLE. I didn't tell her you told me. Just that you gave me a little hint.

WOODY. That's great. [*Shaking her head.*] And now this thing with Griswold—about the picture. What'd you go and start *that* for?

COLE. All I said was it was a good picture. Is there anything wrong with that?

WOODY. I don't dig it, Cole. What are you in this for?

COLE. [*Smiling.*] I'm in the employ of a foreign government.

WOODY. Quit stalling.

COLE. I'm in it for the same thing you are. I think she's making a mistake. I'd like to stop her.

WOODY. But why should *you* care?

COLE. [*Getting up and coming into the room.*] That ought to be an easy one for a smart girl like you.

WOODY. [*After a pause.*] Oh, God. It all adds up. [*Staring at him*.] How long has *this* been going on? Twenty-*five* years?

COLE. No. He's got a few years' seniority on me.

WOODY. Where did it start?

COLE. Jugoslavia. The first time I saw her she was up to her hips in mud in a shell hole. I thought she was a native, got a shot of her. That night the siege broke and she took a bath— came out a blonde from the *Detroit Free Press*.

WOODY. [*Enjoying it*.] Was she a good reporter then?

COLE. The only reporter I ever knew could sit in a poker game, win the biggest pot and still have every guy wondering what she'd be like in bed.

WOODY. How long did it take you to find out?

COLE. [COLE *gives her a look, crosses away*.] I'll write my biography some day. You can read it.

WOODY. Hey, wait a minute, you can't do that to me—leave me with my tongue hanging out. What happened? I've been with her four years and you never turned up. Then all of a sudden, this weekend—

COLE. I'm on an assignment.

WOODY. Just your stuff— [COLE *turns away*.] For God's sake, Cole, I'm not being nosey. I don't just work for this woman. I like her. I care what happens to her.

COLE. [COLE *turns and looks at her for a long moment. He believes her. Quietly*.] I haven't seen her since Paris—August 26, 1944. The day of the liberation. Me and every other newspaper hack in Europe had "liberated" the city—with a little help, of course, from the Allied Forces. I shot two hundred and forty-one pictures by six o'clock and sent them off. Then I went over to the Scribe Bar. The "cream" of American Journalism was there—and all way ahead of me. The place was a madhouse—I wanted to get out fast. [*Pause*.] Then I saw Agatha. I hadn't seen her in six months. She had a red flower in that blonde hair—it stood out against the khaki and smoke. She was talking with some officer. She saw me and she stopped talking—I could tell it was in the middle of a sentence. It took us ten minutes to push our way through to each other, and another five minutes to get outside. That was even more hectic. The French people were celebrating outside—with champagne they'd hoarded in cellars for four years. Men wept in the streets, strangers kissed like lovers. Nobody talked—they yelled. [*He stops, remembering.*] I had to fight off two French Maquis to hang on to Agatha. Then I saw two more coming. I pushed in a door and pulled her after me. It was a barber shop. I could smell the hair tonic when I kissed her. And when I did, I knew it didn't matter that she'd ducked out on me in China—that she'd been a little remote in Algiers. I knew I wasn't going to ask her why—I was just going to ask her to marry me. She knew it, too. She had a room at the Ritz and she gave me the key while she went to her office to file her story. I bought up all the flowers I could find in ten blocks and sent them up to the room. Then I went up. [*Wryly.*] I sprinkled rose petals in the doorway— [*A long pause.*] They were a little brown around the edges when I got the cable from London. It said there'd been an urgent message calling her back to New York. Would I have the hotel send her bag on to her? [*He stops, smiles without humor.*] Well, I did. But I looked in it first. She travelled light. A tooth brush, a clean khaki blouse, a pair of stockings, two cakes of soap, her newspaper credentials, a flashlight—and a snapshot of a man. Not a very good one— overexposed. But good enough for me to remember. I recognized the face last week in a New York newspaper announcing the return of the "Honorable Agatha Reed" to her college for an honorary degree.

WOODY. [WOODY *just looks at him, not saying anything. Finally.*] I'm sorry, Cole.

COLE. What are you sorry about? Now that I've seen him, I'm not worried. He's no competition—he's a memory. Something she's pressed in a book through the years. Like a goddam rose.

WOODY. Maybe you're right, but she doesn't know it.

COLE. She will. She's a realist—she can lie to herself just so much. Then she'll see him for what he is. [*Confidently.*] And then she'll see me.

WOODY. You're expecting a lot from her in just two days.

COLE. Maybe. That's why I'm giving her a little help. A little sleight-of-hand. Something I picked up from an old Hindu fakir. Watch closely now—a word here, a word there—and right before your very eyes, I turn the memory back into—a man.

WOODY. Very clever, if it works.

COLE. It's working already, isn't it? Isn't it?

WOODY. Yes, she's getting worried. [*Suddenly.*] Look, I don't know. Maybe it's better for you to sit back and let the thing happen by itself. Like I am— [*The phone rings.* WOODY *goes to it, picks it up.*] Hello?—Oh. [*She looks at* COLE *for a second.*] All right. Put him through. [*A pause.*] Hello?—Oh, hello, George. Have you got that stuff for me?—Good. That was quick work. [COLE *stretches out on the sofa.*] Just a minute till I get a pencil. [*Picking up pad and pencil.*] All right, George. All set.—What? You're kidding. I don't believe it. On the other hand, maybe I do.—Don't be silly, that's a big help, George. Much obliged.—Yes, and we ought to be back next week. I'll drop in to see you. And thanks again. [*She hangs up, looks at the pad in her hand for a moment meditatively.*]

COLE. Trouble?

WOODY. [*Casually.*] No. Just routine stuff.

COLE. [COLE *sits up, looks straight at her.*] Don't give me those "baby blues." Sit back—see what happens. Butter wouldn't melt in your mouth.

WOODY. Well, I—

COLE. [*Crossing to her.*] You've been busy as a little bee!

WOODY. It's nothing. I just asked a friend to do a little research for me.

COLE. Don't apologize. You're terrific! What research?

WOODY. He looked up Merrill for me.

COLE. What about him?

WOODY. Well, it's mighty interesting. He—

COLE. [*Stopping her.*] Wait a minute—don't tell me. I've got this guy all figured out. He's one of these—

[*There's a sudden squealing outside in the hall.*]

GIRL'S VOICE. [*Off stage.*] Oh, Miss Reed, have some candy!

[*Other* GIRLS' *voices chime in.*]

WOODY. [*Over it.*] That's Agatha. Look, you better get out of here.

COLE. Why?

WOODY. She thinks we're in cahoots as it is. If she sees you in here she'll blow her top.

COLE. [*Crossing to the window.*] Okay.

WOODY. No. They can see that window from the hall. [*Pushing him toward the bedroom.*] There are a couple of windows in there on the other side. Be sure no one sees you climbing out.

COLE. [*As he exits.*] This takes me back to my youth.

[WOODY *closes the bedroom door.* AGATHA *enters, followed by* MARY NELL, CLARISSE, AMELIA, *and* CAROL. *They're all in evening dress, and the* GIRLS *are very excited.* MARY NELL *is holding out a box of candy.*]

MARY NELL. —And I'd consider it a great honor for you to have a piece, Miss Reed.

AGATHA. [*Taking one.*] Why, thank you, Mary Nell.

AMELIA. We didn't even know Mary Nell was going to pass the candy. It was a big surprise.

CLARISSE. Isn't it exciting?

WOODY. I don't get it.

AGATHA. It's an old custom. You pass the candy to announce your engagement.

MARY NELL. Won't you have a piece, Miss Woods?

WOODY. [*Helping herself.*] What does it mean if I take two? Twins?

MARY NELL. Oh, no—

AGATHA. Who's the lucky man?

MARY NELL. Sam Carter. I don't think you know him.

CAROL. I bet she does. He was All-American, 1947.

WOODY. The only All-Americans we know are on a committee.

[*The* GIRLS *look mystified.*]

AGATHA. [*Quickly.*] Where's Ginny? Shouldn't she be in on all this celebration?

MARY NELL. She took some of her stuff home and she isn't back yet. I tried to hold out but I just couldn't. Besides I wanted to tell you. It's all your doing.

AGATHA. My doing?

MARY NELL. Uh huh. You see, last night Sam and I were parked over—[*She stops.*]—were sitting and talking about what I was going to do after graduation. And I said I'd been thinking about it a lot since you came and I thought I might go to Washington and get a job in the Government and then some day I might even run for Congress like you.

WOODY. [*She chokes. Apologetically.*] Candy—

MARY NELL. Sam didn't understand. He laughed. And I got awfully mad. I didn't talk to him all the way home. But then he explained. He said he only laughed because he had other plans for me. Such as asking me to be Mrs. Sam Carter.

AMELIA. Wasn't that darling?

MARY NELL. And we're going to live in Bangor, Maine, and have a wood-burning fireplace in every room practically.

AGATHA. Sounds wonderful.

MARY NELL. [*Expansively.*] Everybody have another piece of candy! [*Passing it, her face sobers.*] Miss Reed. You don't think I made a mistake, do you? Giving up the Government and Congress and all that.

AGATHA. Do you feel as if you've made a mistake?

MARY NELL. No.

AGATHA. Then you haven't. Most mistakes you make you can feel. [*She avoids* WOODY's *piercing glance.*]

MARY NELL. Gosh. I just remembered. This is probably the last time I'll be in this room. [*She looks around, swallowing.*]

CLARISSE. It was always the nicest room in the Dorm.

MARY NELL. Wasn't it? Ginny made the curtains. I was going to make spreads. But I never got to it.

AMELIA. Seems just yesterday we were Freshmen.

CAROL. And tomorrow it'll all be over.

MARY NELL. I can hardly believe it.

[*There's a silent, poignant moment.*]

JO. [*Appearing in the doorway.*] Hey! The men are here!

[*It's electrifying. Lumps in throats are gone, and there's a mad dash for the door. All exit.*]

WOODY. I'll give you one guess what *they* majored in. [*Then.*] How was the interview?

AGATHA. Oh, the usual. Is Congress going to do anything to

stop inflation? Has the United Nations got a chance and how do I feel about the Draft.

WOODY. Did you tell them?

AGATHA. I went easy.

WOODY. Easy? Since when have you started pulling your punches?

AGATHA. Well, after all, I'm not down here for political purposes.

WOODY. I know, but—

AGATHA. Well, I'm not. It would just create more embarrassment—

WOODY. [WOODY *stares at her, then turns abruptly and walks to the desk.*] I finished typing the notes you dictated for your Commencement speech. You better look them over tonight. [*She pulls the sheet out of the typewriter.*]

AGATHA. Good idea. [*She takes the pages, then sets them down absently.*]

WOODY. [*Suddenly making up her mind.*] I have some other notes you might like to look over. [*She picks up her shorthand pad.*]

AGATHA. Other notes?

WOODY. I called George Cameron and asked him to see what dope there might be around on Merrill.

AGATHA. You did—what?

WOODY. Yeah, I'm funny that way. I like to know everything I can about everybody. You always said that's what makes me such a good secretary.

AGATHA. Stop making excuses. It's inexcusable! [*As* WOODY *shrugs and starts to put down the pad.*] What did he find out?

WOODY. [*Handing her the pad.*] It's right here. You can read it.

AGATHA. [*Almost unwillingly* AGATHA *crosses to her, takes the pad. She looks at it, turns over the page, goes back to the first one in confusion.*] I don't understand.

WOODY. Just what you see there.

AGATHA. [*Looking again.*] There's nothing here.

WOODY. That's what I mean. Nothing. An unblemished record. [*As* AGATHA *relaxes.*] That's what bothers me.

AGATHA. Bothers you?

WOODY. Yes. Don't you think it's funny? He's a prominent educator. Yet he's never been a member of one committee that took a stand on any issue. Not a single endorsement of anything the least bit political, controversial. Never even been investigated *once*.

AGATHA. What are you trying to say?

WOODY. We've just been through a war. People took stands on things. *You've* been investigated.

AGATHA. [*Icy.*] Very nice, Woody. Only don't forget. I've seen you work before.

WOODY. For God's sake, Agatha. If you want to get married, it's your own business. I just want you to be happy.

AGATHA. [*With mounting anger.*] What makes you think I won't be?

WOODY. I'm not saying you won't. I'm just asking. After all, you haven't seen this man for twenty years. And now in just two days, you think—

AGATHA. [*Violently.*] I'm *tired* of all this—

GINNY. [GINNY *knocks on the door frame.*] Miss Reed, could I talk to you?

AGATHA. Yes, of course.

[*There is an awkward pause. Then, as* GINNY *enters,* WOODY *starts to the door.*]

WOODY. I forgot to tell you. There's some flowers there for you.

[*She exits.*]

[AGATHA *stands, looking after her. Then, pulling herself together, she turns to* GINNY.]

AGATHA. Shouldn't you be dressed by now? [*She opens the flower box, reads the card.*]

GINNY. I had to drop some things off at my father's house.

AGATHA. [*Lifting out the orchids.*] These are from him. He's my date for the Step-sing and the Prom. And he's late.

GINNY. Yes, I know. They're having a meeting over there.

AGATHA. [*Looks at her.*] A meeting?

GINNY. Yes. [*Abruptly.*] Is it a good picture? The one you brought down?

AGATHA. Yes, I think it is.

GINNY. Would you call it—propaganda?

AGATHA. It's a picture against war. If that's propaganda, it's like propaganda against cancer. [*Quietly.*] Why, Ginny?

GINNY. Nothing.

AGATHA. What are you trying to tell me?

GINNY. [*Facing her.*] Some people think the President of a college has the right to make decisions on things. But he doesn't. He has to check everything with the trustees. Whatever he may feel himself, that doesn't matter.

AGATHA. You mean, they may not show the movie?

GINNY. [*Fervently.*] It's like you said yourself. Being President is different from just being a professor. You have more responsibility, so you have to make more concessions. He's done wonderful things for the school. Seven new buildings in ten years. And last year they named him the most successful college administrator east of the Rockies. Isn't that something to be proud of? I'm so proud I could— [*She turns away, fighting back the sobs. They come anyway—the dam finally run over.*]

AGATHA. [*She crosses to her.*] It's all right, Ginny. It's all right.

GINNY. I'm so ashamed. I've been ashamed for a long time now.

[*She starts blindly for the door.*]

AGATHA. Where are you going?

GINNY. I don't know. Anywhere—away from here—

AGATHA. [*Catching her.*] Stop it, Ginny! Stop it!

GINNY. Why? Why should I stay? To stand up there and let him hand me a diploma when I know it doesn't mean anything?

AGATHA. That's not so. It's yours for what you've learned here.

GINNY. What have I learned? That my father's a coward? That he's so afraid of losing his job he's lost everything else he ever believed in? Oh, I've made apologies. I've made them till I can't look at him any more. But there've been too many things. [*Pulling away.*] Dr. Pitt wasn't the first, and your movie won't be the last.

AGATHA. Wait, Ginny. You may be wrong.

GINNY. I'm not wrong.

AGATHA. When you left the house, had they finished? Had they decided not to show the picture?

GINNY. No, but—

AGATHA. Then how do you know? How do you know he hasn't fought them on this?

GINNY. He's forgotten how to fight.

AGATHA. Sometimes a man needs a certain moment. Maybe this is it.

GINNY. I can't listen any more, Miss Reed. I can't—

[*She starts for the door, but* AGATHA *catches her arm and holds her.*]

AGATHA. Ginny, you must listen! You probably know I was expelled from this college. I want you to know why. Because I stayed out all night with a man. We were very much in love— we were planning to be married. But I ran away—so I wouldn't hurt his chances of becoming President. [GINNY's *face pales.*] Even at eighteen, I felt it was important for a man like him to be the President of a college. I think your father remembers that today. Whatever's happened in between, I think he'd like to be that man again. [GINNY *crosses away from her.*] Maybe you resent me now. That was the chance I had to take. But I want you to know why I told you this. It's because I've grown very fond of you. You have a good mind and a whole life ahead of you. You mustn't throw it away by being bitter and disillusioned. [*There's a long moment.* AGATHA *turns away in defeat.*]

GINNY. I don't resent you. [AGATHA *wheels.*] I think I just grew up a little, though.

AGATHA. I'm sorry.

GINNY. Don't be. It's good. I should have known. Whenever he talked about you, he was different. That's why Uncle Willy — It's been in his study ever since I can remember.

AGATHA. [*Encouraged herself.*] I didn't know.

GINNY. [*Suddenly smiling.*] I feel better. I feel so much better.

[*The telephone rings.* AGATHA *crosses to answer it.*]

AGATHA. [*Into telephone.*] Hello— Yes, this is Miss Reed. Will you ask Dr. Merrill to come in, please? [*She hangs up.* GINNY *has started for the door.*] Where are you going?

GINNY. Don't worry. Just to get dressed.

AGATHA. Good.

GINNY. [*Turning.*] I want you to know, I never gave him up, really. I just needed someone else to believe in him, too. [*She goes out.*]

[AGATHA *hurries across the room to her flower box. She's tense, expectant. She fumbles putting the flower on, sticks herself, finally gets it. There's a knock on the door. She turns, takes a deep breath.*]

AGATHA. Come in. [*The door opens and* MERRILL *stands there. He's in tails, exceedingly distinguished and exceedingly handsome.* AGATHA *smiles.*] I'd begun to feel jilted. As if—

[*There is a strident, hysterical giggle from the corridor.*]

MERRILL. [*Apologetically.*] Claude and Ellen dropped by. They thought we might as well make it a foursome.

[*The* GRISWOLDS *enter behind him.* CLAUDE GRISWOLD *is a personable, jovial man in his late forties. He wears an impeccable tuxedo. He also wears the indefinable air which a great deal of money and power give to a man. Too many people have told Claude Griswold he's right for him ever again to believe that he's wrong.* ELLEN *wears an evening gown that seems carefully designed to accentuate all the worst points of her figure—the kind that always costs a lot of money. She has obviously kept up the pace from the afternoon's cocktail party because by now she's really sailing.*]

ELLEN. Just like old times, Ag. [*To* CLAUDE.] We always went on double dates.

GRISWOLD. Well, how do we stack up against the 1928 wolves?

ELLEN. They had more hair.

GRISWOLD. But less money, eh, Jim?

MERRILL. Speak for yourself, Claude.

GRISWOLD. Now, don't let him give you the impression education doesn't pay, Miss Reed. I know. I sign his checks. [*At*

MERRILL's *obvious discomfort.*] Don't get embarrassed, Jim. It's worth every cent to have a President who can wear tails like that.

ELLEN. Claude could wear them too, but he just won't.

GRISWOLD. They flap against my legs.

ELLEN. That's silly. If you were too short, I could understand it. [*Suddenly.*] Ag, remember the buzzer? [*To the men.*] You could buzz from the lounge to the rooms. When one of us had a blind date, the other always went in first. One buzz—he was short, low heels. Two buzzes, tall—high heels. [*Looking at* CLAUDE *complacently.*] Remember, I always said I'd marry a two-buzz.

GRISWOLD. I've been called a lot of things in my time—

MERRILL. You seem full of reminiscences tonight, Ellen.

GRISWOLD. And martinis.

ELLEN. I guess it's being back in the old room with Uncle Willy —and Ag and everything. [*The remote sound of instruments tuning up floats through the open window.*] Oh, listen, the orchestra's warming up. [*Her eye catches the victrola.*] We've got to warm up, too.

GRISWOLD. Now, Ellen, there's plenty of time—

ELLEN. Now, don't be a kill-joy. [*Picking up a record.*] Stan Kenton. He's super. Isn't that the word now? [*She puts the record on.*]

GRISWOLD. Ellen, we're going to be dancing all evening.

ELLEN. Oh, come on. [*She sways up to him—her arms outstretched.*]

GRISWOLD. This is silly.

ELLEN. It's awful to be married to a man with no imagination. [*That does it.* GRISWOLD *grasps his wife firmly and swings her into a fox trot.*] Where's your manners, Jim? Aren't you going to ask Ag to dance?

[MERRILL *looks at* AGATHA *helplessly.*]

GRISWOLD. [*Puffing a bit.*] Every year dance music keeps— getting—faster and faster.

ELLEN. Could be you're just getting slower and slower.

GRISWOLD. [*He stops, puffing slightly.*] Can't do it— I'm out of condition.

AGATHA. [*Gratefully.*] I think we're all out of condition. [*She takes advantage of the opportunity to cross and turn off the victrola.*]

GRISWOLD. [*Pressing his chest.*] Besides, I ate too fast tonight.

ELLEN. Well, it's your own fault. [*Irritably.*] If we hadn't had to rush off and see that movie in the middle of everything— [*She stops herself.*]

[MERRILL *and* GRISWOLD *exchange glances.* AGATHA'S *back is turned. There is a silent, strained moment. Then she turns slowly.*]

AGATHA. Too bad. Sounds like it's all my fault.

ELLEN. Oh, I didn't mean that, Ag. I just meant— [*She looks helplessly at her husband.*]

AGATHA. [*Crossing to* GRISWOLD.] How did you like the picture?

GRISWOLD. Well—it's no Abbott and Costello.

ELLEN. They're Claude's favorites.

MERRILL. Don't you think we ought to get along now? It's getting rather late. [*It's obvious he's trying to avoid a discussion.*]

AGATHA. [*She makes up her mind.*] Don't rush us, Jim. We've plenty of time. The Seniors aren't even out on the steps yet.

Besides, this is the first time I've had a chance to talk with Mr. Griswold.

GRISWOLD. Make it Claude.

AGATHA. Claude. I haven't even had a moment to compliment you on all the signs of your interest around the campus. The motion picture machine, for instance. How did it occur to you?

GRISWOLD. Well, I'd like to take credit for that, but it was really Jim's idea.

MERRILL. Visual education's been one of our pet projects for a long time.

GRISWOLD. Jim's got to make it sound important. But what made me reach my hand in my pocket was the thought of the kick those kids were going to get, seeing movies right on campus.

ELLEN. It's a good thing you haven't got a daughter. She'd be spoiled silly.

GRISWOLD. I've got six hundred and twenty-two daughters. *All* spoiled silly. And why not? They've got time enough to start worrying their heads when they're *out* of college.

AGATHA. That's an interesting theory of education.

GRISWOLD. No. I leave the theories to the experts like Jim here. I just know what I like and what I don't like.

AGATHA. [*Doggedly.*] Which brings us back to what you thought of the picture.

MERRILL. [*Quickly.*] Well, of course, Claude understands what you're trying to do with this picture.

GRISWOLD. It's a good thing to make pictures like this about outlawing war. As long as—

AGATHA. Nobody sees them? [*There's something in her tone.*]

GRISWOLD. [GRISWOLD *looks at her, laughs.*] I was going to say as long as you're careful who you show them to. For instance, if I'd known some of those strong scenes were going to be in that picture, I wouldn't have wanted Ellen here to see it.

ELLEN. It's all right, Claude. I turned my head away at the bad parts.

AGATHA. That's a shame, Ellen. They're worth seeing and remembering.

ELLEN. I just meant—

GRISWOLD. Don't forget, you're a very special kind of woman, Miss Reed. You've been out on the field, on the war fronts. You've gotten a kind of toughness about this sort of thing. More like—well, more like a man.

AGATHA. I'm sure you intended that as a compliment.

MERRILL. Miss Reed, you realize what Claude meant was—

AGATHA. —That I'm a very superior woman because I can face ugly things without turning my head away. But those other poor creatures, the rest of my sex, we must be very careful to spare them. Because they have such delicate stomachs.

GRISWOLD. Well, haven't they?

AGATHA. What do you think of that description of women, Ellen?

[ELLEN *looks from* AGATHA *to her husband in disturbed bewilderment.*]

GRISWOLD. Miss Reed, I'm a great admirer of yours—even if we don't always agree politically. I say thank God we've got the right to disagree with each other here in this country. But I don't like propaganda—

MERRILL. [*Crossing to him.*] Claude!

GRISWOLD. [*Resolutely.*] —whether it's from Congresswomen, or scientists or the President of the United States!

AGATHA. That's become such an easy word. Is it propaganda to show that the results of another war will be the most devastating the world's ever known?

GRISWOLD. There's too much scaremongering going on. All these scientists getting hot under the collar. All this loose talk. You're not going to stop wars that way.

AGATHA. How *are* you going to stop them?

GRISWOLD. There've always been wars. There always will be. It's human nature and we may as well face it.

AGATHA. [*Something explodes inside her.*] You own Great Northern Textiles, don't you? [GRISWOLD *faces her.*] I sit on the Jameson Committee. We've been reviewing war profits.

GRISWOLD. [*With a steady smile.*] What are you trying to say, Miss Reed? That I made money out of the war? Sure I did. So did everyone. I'd have been a fool not to. But if you're accusing me of doing anything to start another war—

AGATHA. No, Mr. Griswold, I don't believe that. But what are you doing to stop another one?

GRISWOLD. That's beyond my power.

AGATHA. Maybe. Maybe it's really in the power of your six hundred and twenty-two daughters. But only if they know what war means. If they look at it—if they understand it.

GRISWOLD. You mean, cheat these kids out of their youth? No, sir! Life's tough enough. Let them have these few years of fun instead of drumming their heads full of war—

AGATHA. And then just hand them one and say—don't understand it. Fight it. Die for it.

GRISWOLD. [*Admiringly.*] Miss Reed, I can understand why you start so much fireworks down there in Congress. But it all boils down to one thing. *We* know what's best for our school—

MERRILL. [*Warningly.*] Claude—

GRISWOLD. Now, let's stop this beating around the bush, Jim.

MERRILL. [*Desperately.*] Claude, if you'll just let me handle this—

GRISWOLD. There's no handling to it. [MERRILL *crosses away from them.*] I like to be frank, Miss Reed. We've cancelled the showing of the film—the trustees took a vote an hour ago. There'll be a statement that the schedule got overcrowded. [*There's a pause.*]

AGATHA. I see. [*She turns to* MERRILL.] And the President, did he agree?

[MERRILL'S *face is strained. He starts to say something, but* GRISWOLD *says it for him.*]

GRISWOLD. The President and the trustees always agree. [AGATHA *looks at* MERRILL, *waiting for him to deny it. He doesn't.*] I'm sorry this had to happen, Miss Reed. Nothing personal in it at all. I hope it won't spoil an extremely pleasant weekend.

MERRILL. Claude, I'd like to speak to Miss Reed alone.

GRISWOLD. Now, stop worrying, Jim. You're making too much of this thing. Miss Reed's a sensible woman.

MERRILL. [*Insistently.*] We'll join you.

GRISWOLD. [*Annoyed.*] All right. Only, don't be too long. It wouldn't look well if you were late— [*It's an order. He turns to* ELLEN.] Come on, Ellen. [*For the first time in her marriage,* ELLEN *looks at her husband with the suspicion that he may be less than perfect. She looks back at* AGATHA. *Then, quietly, she exits.* GRISWOLD *bows to* AGATHA.] Miss Reed. [*He exits, closes the door.*]

[*It seems very still for a moment.*]

AGATHA. I feel a little—sick.

MERRILL. Agatha, you're not giving me a chance to explain.

AGATHA. Did you feel that movie shouldn't be shown?

MERRILL. It wasn't a question of—

AGATHA. Be frank with me, Jim. Did you think it was wrong for your Seniors to see?

MERRILL. [*After a struggle.*] No.

AGATHA. And you didn't stand up and say that?

MERRILL. Agatha, you're not being very objective. I know it's embarrassing for you to bring a film down here—

AGATHA. [*Aghast.*] Could you possibly believe my vanity is concerned in this?

MERRILL. I didn't say that. I'm just asking you to try and see my position. I can't always bluster through my own opinions. There are moments when I have to bow to—

AGATHA. Claude?

MERRILL. You're exaggerating Claude's whole importance in this affair.

AGATHA. Am I? When he, not you, seems to be the real judge of what should be taught in this college. By what right? Do you respect him as an educator?

MERRILL. He doesn't pretend to be that. He's a business man. And a very successful one.

AGATHA. Fine, but a college isn't a business.

MERRILL. Then who's going to pay for it? Don't forget, he's the man who foots the bills. And he's very generous.

AGATHA. Yes, I know. Give a college a Science building—then tell the professors what they can say in it. Give them a motion picture machine but tell them what to run on it. That's not generosity. That's an investment—with damned good dividends!

MERRILL. All right. It's a business deal. He gives money. He wants his say. It's as simple as that. [*At* AGATHA's *look.*] Why do you look so shocked?

AGATHA. Not shocked. Frightened. That *you* stand here and say that, and *accept* it.

MERRILL. Good God, Agatha, I have to run a college. That means I have to get money, endowments, buildings. It's part of the job. So I've learned to compromise. I give in on smaller things here and there so I can win on larger ones.

AGATHA. [*Facing him.*] What *are* the larger ones? Or have you been waiting for them so long you don't recognize them anymore?

MERRILL. You mean Dr. Pitt? This film? Suppose I fought Griswold on them? To a showdown. It would be a heroic gesture. But I'd be out of here tomorrow.

AGATHA. Would you? You used to fight very well.

MERRILL. [*Slight pause.*] Things are quite different now. I have Ginny to think of.

AGATHA. You don't know your daughter very well, do you, Jim?

MERRILL. We have a very good relationship.

AGATHA. There's no need to lie to me. I've seen you together.

MERRILL. [*Turning away.*] I don't care to discuss it any more.

AGATHA. You've got to discuss it. You've got a bigger stake in this than you think. [*He wheels, looks at her.*] You're going to lose her, Jim. I don't know how important that is to you. I suspect it's very important.

MERRILL. [*Angrily.*] What have you been telling her?

AGATHA. Terrible things. That you have courage. That you have integrity. [MERRILL *turns away to the window. She knows she's reaching him.*] I didn't just say it. I believe it, Jim: Stand up to Griswold. Not for me. Not even for Ginny. For yourself.

[*There is a poignant silence.* AGATHA *can see the struggle mirrored in his back. Suddenly there's a sharp knock on the door. Neither of them moves. The knock repeats.*]

CAROL. [*Offstage.*] Dr. Merrill. [MERRILL *crosses, opens the door.*] Mr. Griswold sent me, Dr. Merrill. They're waiting for you and Miss Reed.

[*Just the name does it. The name and all the years of acquiescence. You can see it happen. In one long moment.*]

MERRILL. We'll be right there.

CAROL. I'll tell him. [*She disappears.*]

[AGATHA *has sunk into a chair, her face white, like a woman who's been slapped.*]

MERRILL. We'd better go. [*She's quiet.*] We're late.

AGATHA. You've jumped through the hoop too long, haven't you?

MERRILL. [*Harshly.*] Are you coming?

AGATHA. In a moment. I have a few more things to say.

MERRILL. Agatha, I'm sorry, but there's no use in pursuing the matter any—

AGATHA. [*Rising.*] Oh, I'm not going to plead with you any more. No more appeals to your better nature. I know when I'm licked. [*She smiles.*] I'm going to make a deal with you. A business deal. That's more in your line.

MERRILL. What are you talking about?

AGATHA. A few minutes ago I assured your daughter that you'd run this picture tomorrow. I don't like to think of her finding out that you won't. So I'm afraid you're going to do it. With or without Mr. Griswold's consent. I'll leave procedure up to you.

MERRILL. Is this your idea of a joke?

AGATHA. —And in exchange for that small service, I'll give you my personal guarantee that the *Life* article won't even hint at the colorful events leading up to my expulsion from this seat of higher learning. [MERRILL *stares at her.*] You can imagine how excited Cole would be, stumbling across such a juicy morsel. Such a beautiful tale of love and sacrifice. A daring young girl caught climbing in her dormitory window—see picture of window on preceding page—braving the perils of expulsion rather than blight the budding career of her lover. And now, twenty years later—the girl, a Congresswoman, asked back to her college for an honorary degree. And the lover—hold on to your hats now, folks—the President of the college!

MERRILL. I can't believe you'd—

AGATHA. Why not? You see, I'm willing to take a chance on you, Jim. I know now that you're a coward, and with a coward it's only a question of the lesser of two evils. Whether you *risk being removed from here by running the picture or whether* you accept the *certainty* of being removed when this story breaks.

MERRILL. You'd really do a thing like this?

AGATHA. Yes. You learn all kinds of dirty tricks in my work. The most important one being never to play fair except when you respect the men you're playing with. [*She picks up her scarf from the chair.*]

[*From outside, the clear young voices of the Senior Class have broken into the Alma Mater as the step-sing obviously begins.*]

VOICES. [*Off.*]

"Good Hope, Our Alma Mater
  Thy wisdom and thy truth
  Shall grow forever greater
  In the years beyond our youth—

AGATHA. The Alma Mater. Appropriate, isn't it?

VOICES. [*Off.*]

"Whate'er may be our station,
  Whate'er the storm and strife—

[MERRILL *stands there for a second. Then he turns without a word and goes out.*]

> "Thy shining inspiration
> Shall light our way through life—

[AGATHA *looks after him. Then she walks slowly to the door, turns off the lights and exits. The room is in darkness except for the moonlight streaming in the windows.*]

> "So we raise up our voices and we shout Good Hope,
> Good old Good Hope—
> All the praise of our voices is about Good Hope,
> Good old Good Hope—

[*The bedroom door opens, and* COLE *comes out. There is a calm satisfaction about even his silhouette which makes it obvious that he hasn't missed a word.*]

> "We hope to be
> Worthy of thee
> And we plight love undying
> To thy bright colors flying
> In our hearts, brave and bold—

[COLE *lights a cigarette and starts slowly across the stage toward the window.*]

> "Maroon and Gold—
> Good old—
> GOOD HOPE!

THE CURTAIN HAS FALLEN

ACT THREE

PHOTO BY VANDAMM

ACT THREE

SCENE: *It's early the next afternoon. Half an hour before the Commencement procession is scheduled to start.*
The room looks much the same except for a bed pillow crushed at one end of the sofa, and on the table an ash tray spilling over with cigarette butts.
WOODY *is alone in the room and on the telephone.*

WOODY. [*Into telephone.*] —No, I think it would be better if we drove into Boston and made that seven o'clock plane. That would get us back to Washington tonight. See if you can arrange that.—Good. [*She hangs up, takes a few papers from the desk and puts them in her open briefcase. The telephone rings. She picks it up.*] Hello?— No, she's not back yet, Miss Shackleford. I haven't seen her since eight o'clock.—I really don't know. She just said she was going for a walk. [*She puts the telephone down as* MISS SHACKLEFORD *continues talking, locks the type-writer case, then picks the telephone up again.*] Yes, I know the procession starts in half an hour. I'm sure she does, too— Yes, all right. [*She hangs up, takes her typewriter case from the desk, crosses to Center and sets it down beside the chair. She continues on toward the bedroom, singing "Goodbye, My Alma Mater—"* WOODY *gives every appearance of a happy woman as she exits into the bedroom. In a moment,* MISS BIRDESHAW *appears in the doorway and looks around timidly. She's in a cap and gown and seems a little pale around the edges. Hesitantly, she steps into the room.*]

MISS BIRDESHAW. Anybody here?

WOODY. [*Offstage.*] Agatha? I've been worrying about— [*As she enters, carrying Agatha's small suitcase.*] Oh, it's *you.*

MISS BIRDESHAW. The door was open. So I just came on in. [*Timidly.*] Is Miss Reed back yet?

WOODY. No.

MISS BIRDESHAW. Do you mind if I wait?

WOODY. [*Setting down Agatha's suitcase.*] *I* don't mind, if you don't.

[MISS BIRDESHAW *sits down on the sofa with a minimum of disturbance as* WOODY *crosses toward the desk.*]

MISS BIRDESHAW. I hope Agatha's feelings aren't hurt. I didn't get to her film showing this morning. I had a little—ah, headache.

WOODY. [*With grim satisfaction.*] Didn't you know? The film showing was cancelled last night. [*She drops Agatha's wilted corsage of the night before in the waste basket.*]

MISS BIRDESHAW. Oh, I'm glad. [*Hastily.*] I mean, I'm glad I didn't miss it. [*After a slight pause.*] I—I don't think I got to say goodnight to you yesterday at the tea, Miss Woods.

WOODY. Not in so many words.

MISS BIRDESHAW. I—I had to leave early.

WOODY. Kind of early.

MISS BIRDESHAW. Did I leave with anyone? I mean— [*Swallowing.*] It was very nice of Professor Dingley to accompany me—wasn't it?

WOODY. [WOODY *turns, amused, suddenly understanding what* MISS BIRDESHAW *is worrying about.*] Very. He wouldn't let anyone else carry you.

MISS BIRDESHAW. *Carry* me?

[WOODY *nods.* MISS BIRDESHAW *emits a little moan.*]

WOODY. You felt a little—sleepy. We took you home.

MISS BIRDESHAW. We? *You* undressed me?

WOODY. Yes.

MISS BIRDESHAW. [*Sinking back with a sigh of relief.*] Thank you, Miss Woods.

WOODY. Not at all. Some day you can return the favor.

MISS BIRDESHAW. I must have acted pretty silly yesterday.

WOODY. Don't you remember?

MISS BIRDESHAW. I remember some things.

WOODY. You told some great stories. About your Aunt Deborah. The time she locked herself in the carriage house all night with two of the stable boys—

MISS BIRDESHAW. Oh, no! [*Faintly.*] Did Professor Dingley laugh at that?

WOODY. He choked. That was when you took him out in the garden for some deep breaths of fresh air. Do you remember that?

MISS BIRDESHAW. A little. [*Blushing.*] I suppose I ought to be ashamed of myself.

WOODY. Why?

MISS BIRDESHAW. At my age— [*Then, remembering.*] But I had a wonderful time. The best time I ever had in my life.

WOODY. [*Touched.*] Good. That's the way to talk.

MISS BIRDESHAW. I wonder—maybe you'd tell Agatha I'm sorry. In case she feels badly about yesterday. I've been worrying about that.

WOODY. Sure, I'll tell her.

MISS BIRDESHAW. Thank you. Then I think I'll run along. [*Rising.*] Professor Dingley's waiting for me outside. We're walking in the procession together, you know.

WOODY. No, I didn't.

MISS BIRDESHAW. He dropped by this morning, to see how I felt. He brought me some roses—yellow roses. Two dozen.

WOODY. That was very thoughtful.

MISS BIRDESHAW. Wasn't it? [*Then.*] Do you know something,

Miss Woods? Professor Dingley and I have walked in twenty-three Commencement processions at this college. But this is the first time we'll have ever walked—together.

[*She smiles at* WOODY, *her eyes bright, her cheeks flushed.* MISS BIRDESHAW *looks almost pretty.* MISS SHACKLEFORD *bustles in.*]

MISS SHACKLEFORD. Is Agatha back yet?

WOODY. Not yet.

MISS SHACKLEFORD. My goodness, I hope she realizes what time it— [*She notices* MISS BIRDESHAW.] Oh.

MISS BIRDESHAW. I—I had some business with Miss Reed.

MISS SHACKLEFORD. I see. [*She crosses past* MISS BIRDESHAW *to* WOODY.]

MISS BIRDESHAW. [*Timidly—the old reflex.*] Miss Shackleford, I—uh—

MISS SHACKLEFORD. [*Ignoring her, to* WOODY.] You don't suppose anything—

WOODY. Look, she's got the best attendance record in Congress! [*Indicating the papers on her desk.*] There's her Commencement speech.

MISS SHACKLEFORD. [*Convinced.*] Well, then maybe you can explain to her. We've made a very important change in the procession formation. Her honor guard will come to pick her up *here*. They'll escort her to the Ivy Arch rather than Hope Hall gate. Which means that they'll *follow* the President and the Dean instead of *preceding* them. Is that clear?

WOODY. Perfectly.

MISS SHACKLEFORD. Good. Now— [*She notices* MISS BIRDESHAW *still standing there.*] Hadn't you better run along, Miss Birdeshaw? The Associate Professors are starting to form right now.

MISS BIRDESHAW. I think I should tell you, Miss Shackleford. [*Quietly.*] Professor Dingley and I are walking together in the procession.

MISS SHACKLEFORD. [*Aghast.*] Why, that's ridiculous, Miss Birdeshaw! You know the full professors are always *several hundred* feet—

MISS BIRDESHAW. —ahead of the associate professors. Yes, I know. But Professor Dingley and I prefer it the other way. And there's no rule that says we can't. [MISS SHACKLEFORD'S *mouth is open.* MISS BIRDESHAW *turns at the door.*] I looked it up. [*She exits.*]

MISS SHACKLEFORD. [*She stares after her.*] Well, I'll certainly be glad when *this* weekend is over!

WOODY. It had its moments.

MISS SHACKLEFORD. Everyone's been acting so strangely. I just don't understand it. First Dr. Merrill, and now Miss Birdeshaw, of all people—

WOODY. Dr. Merrill?

MISS SHACKLEFORD. Yes, with that whole film business. Last night he tells me to cancel it. Then this morning at half past nine he calls and says I'm to go ahead.

WOODY. [*Dumbfounded.*] You mean—Dr. Merrill ordered the film shown?

MISS SHACKLEFORD. Yes. [*Sighing.*] And then Mr. Griswold, calling me up and barking at me like that. As I told him, this is not *my* responsibility. I just do what the President tells me. Really, it's been extremely difficult for me. Now if Commencement goes off without the speakers' platform collapsing or something— [WOODY *is a picture of incredulity and disappointment, but* MISS SHACKLEFORD *hardly notices.* COLE *appears in the doorway.*] Oh, Mr. Cole, did you get what you needed at the film showing?

COLE. Just what I needed, Miss Shackleford.

MISS SHACKLEFORD. Well, thank goodness for you. It's such a comfort to have *someone* going around doing his job. [*As* COLE *leans over and smells the corsage she is wearing.*] Sweet, aren't they?

COLE. [*In high spirits.*] Lovely! You look wonderful, Miss Shackleford. Is that a new hat?

MISS SHACKLEFORD. [*Overcome.*] Oh no, it's—

COLE. It's beautiful. Miss Shackleford, don't you be surprised if you wind up on the cover of *Life!*

MISS SHACKLEFORD. Oh, come now, Mr. Cole! You're pulling my leg.

COLE. No, but it's an idea.

MISS SHACKLEFORD. [*Gulping.*] Why, Mr. Cole— [*She exits in a flurry of embarrassment.*]

COLE. [*Turning to* WOODY.] I *love* that dame.

WOODY. [*Looking at him narrowly.*] Wait a minute—didn't you just come from the film showing?

COLE. Mm-hm.

WOODY. Then what the hell are you so happy about?

COLE. I'm not happy. I'm sad. But—I'm philosophical. Something I learned from—

WOODY AND COLE. [*Together.*] An old Hindu fakir—yeah!

WOODY. The same jerk who taught you to turn a memory into a man?

COLE. What do you want me to do—go around dragging my tail? That's the way it goes. Got to take the bad with the good. You're up—you're down—

SUSAN. [*Hurrying in.*] Oh, Miss Woods—

PHOTO BY A. BENDER

WOODY. Yeah. Anything?

SUSAN. Well, I asked around. Like you said. Casual. And Kip Martin—she was picking up her mother at the railroad station, and she thinks she saw Miss Reed—at least it looked like Miss Reed, walking along the road.

WOODY. When was that?

SUSAN. About an hour ago.

WOODY. [*Starts her toward the door.*] Okay. Good work but keep on asking. See if anyone's seen her since then.

SUSAN. Casual—?

WOODY. That's right. Real casual. [SUSAN *exits.* WOODY *stalks around, troubled.*] An hour ago! I don't like it. *She* sits up all night. *He* runs the picture. And *you're* philosophical. There's something fishy about all this. I don't know— [*She looks across at* COLE. *He shrugs. She comes to a decision.*] I'm not going to wait— I'm going to go out and find her myself. [*She exits.*]

COLE. [*His unconcerned pose disappears. He hurries across to the telephone. Into telephone.*] Hello, get me the railroad station.—Yeah—ticket office. [*A pause.*] Hello? Has a tall blonde bought a ticket to anywhere in the past hour?—I see. Are you the only ticket clerk?—So you'd know. Well, thanks. [*He hangs up, starts meditatively across the room. The telephone rings. He wheels and races back to it.*] Hello.—No, Miss Woods just stepped out. But you can give me the message. [*Injured.*] —Oh, you can trust me— Yeah, I got it. Coming through the Ivy Arch. About five minutes ago— Well, that's great work, Casual. I'll see that you're mentioned for a citation. [*He hangs up, looks out the window. She isn't in sight yet. Then, like an expectant lover examining the scene of a rendezvous, he looks around the room. Crossing to the door, he opens it a bit wider. As he wheels, he sees the Clara Bow doll on the radiator shelf. Violently he turns its face to the wall. On the sofa, he sees the crumpled bedpillow. With an attempt at neat-*

ness, he picks it up and tosses it through the bedroom door. His eye falls on the victrola—it's an idea. Background music. He drops the needle on the record, starts away. The voice of Betty Boop oozes out in one of her coyest boop-boop-a-doops. He stops, pained, goes back, takes the record off, breaks it. Searching through a stack of records, he finds a more suitable love song, puts it on—low. As he wanders back across the room, surveying his handiwork with pleasure, he notices a vase of roses. A reminiscent smile lights his face. Taking out a couple of the roses, he tears off the petals and strews a handful in the doorway. Pleased, he continues a path of rose petals to the window seat where he plumps up a pillow and stretches out comfortably, awaiting AGATHA'S *imminent arrival. In a moment, she enters. She's tense and jittery, doesn't even notice the rose petals. Crossing to the mantel, she leans her head against it wearily.* COLE *sits up—watches her for a few seconds.*]

COLE. Tired?

AGATHA. [*She starts at the sound of his voice, turns around.*] What are you doing here?

COLE. Woody went out to look for you. Asked me to stick around in case the phone rang.

AGATHA. Oh.

COLE. [*Rising.*] Well—what's new? [AGATHA *turns away from him. He tries a different tack.*] Heard about the film showing?

AGATHA. Yes. I just met Ginny outside. She told me how— wonderful it was.

COLE. Congratulations. [*She doesn't say anything.*] What's the matter? Aren't you glad?

AGATHA. [*Trying.*] Yes, of course.

COLE. [*Crossing to her.*] Seems you were right about Merrill. Weren't you?

AGATHA. [*Crossing away from him.*] Really, there's no need
to—

COLE. Eat crow? Oh, I don't mind. Where you're concerned,
I've got no pride. You ought to know that by now. I gave it
up when I came down here. [*Approaching her again.*] Of
course, I did have a feeling you might like it—

AGATHA. [*Eluding him again.*] We went through all this
yesterday.

COLE. [*Coming around to face her.*] I know. But that was so
long ago. I thought you might have changed your mind.

AGATHA. Why should I?

COLE. [*Gently.*] People do. All the time. [*Brushing his face
against her hair.*] Besides, I once saw it in a movie—how the
bride turned at the last moment and ran off with the best man.

AGATHA. [*For one moment,* AGATHA *stands there. Then she
breaks away from him.*] Cole, leave me alone—

COLE. [*There is a pause as* COLE *looks at her, unable to believe
that she isn't going to tell him the truth.*] You mean—you've
got nothing to say to me?

AGATHA. I thought we said it all.

COLE. [*Slowly.*] Yeah, but I'm stupid. I've got to have it spelled
out for me. He's a great guy. He's all you've dreamed about—
waited for—for twenty years. You're gonna go right ahead and
marry him—?

AGATHA. [*Her back to him.*] The date hasn't been set—yet.

COLE. But it will be?

AGATHA. [*Turning—desperately.*] I don't see that this is any
of your business!

COLE. You don't? [*Abruptly, he crosses, turns off the victrola.
Then he strides to the telephone, picks it up.*] Get me Dr. Merrill's office.

AGATHA. What are you doing?

COLE. I'm gonna ask Merrill to come over here. I'd like to congratulate him. [*Into telephone.*] Is Dr. Merrill there? I'd like to talk to him— [AGATHA *runs across the room and wrenches the telephone out of his hand, slams it down on the desk.* COLE *stands looking at her.*] You couldn't face that, could you? Because you know it's a lie. You threw away six years we could have had together because of a lie, but you can't be honest enough now to admit it to me. You've got to hang on to your precious ego. Well, you can keep it. I'm a big boy now. I've got bigger and better things to do with my life. [*He turns and goes out.*]

[AGATHA *stands motionless for a moment, her face white, fighting for control. The telephone squeaks "Hello— Hello"— She picks up the receiver and bangs it back on the hook. Lying on the desk beside the telephone is her Commencement speech. She picks it up, reads the first few lines. In her face you can see the disgust at what she's reading. She crumples it violently and throws it into the waste basket. At almost the same moment her eye falls on her suitcase. She stares at it, then makes an impulsive decision, crosses and opens it. It's packed. She shuts it and hurries into the bedroom.* MERRILL *appears in the corridor doorway. He's in his gown, the colors of his degrees rich against the black.* AGATHA *comes hurrying out of the bedroom, carrying her jacket, her hat and purse. She's about to pick up the suitcase when she sees* MERRILL *and stops. He looks at her, taking in her obvious intent.*]

MERRILL. Where are you going?

AGATHA. I can't stay here and go through with this lie any more. I can't.

MERRILL. You realize what you're doing?

AGATHA. Yes. There's my speech in the waste basket—where it belongs. I couldn't get up there and say it. I'd choke on every word! [*She picks up the bag and starts for the door.*] I'll send you a telegram. That I'm sick. Or that I'm needed in Washington. You can read it.

MERRILL. [*Quietly.*] Just like twenty years ago, isn't it, Agatha? [*She stops abruptly.*] Running away again.

AGATHA. [*The effect of his words can be seen in her back. And when she turns to him, it's obvious that she's moved.*] Jim, you don't understand. I was wrong last night—to expect you to be the same man I remembered. Nothing stays the same. And I was wrong to think I could "save" your daughter. I can't blackmail you for the rest of your life. It's better for her to know the truth—now, while she's young.

MERRILL. Would you tell her that?

AGATHA. If I had to, yes.

MERRILL. You'll have your chance. I just saw her running across the Quad. [*There's a knock on the door.*] She's probably there now.

[*The knock comes again.*]

GINNY'S VOICE. It's Ginny.

MERRILL. You'd better answer.

AGATHA. [*Setting down her suitcase quickly and putting her other things on a chair.*] Come in.

GINNY. [GINNY *enters. There are no words to describe her radiance. She smiles at* AGATHA, *then at her father, and it shines out of her.*] I went to your office. They told me you'd come here. [*Crossing to* MERRILL.] We just saw the picture. I wish you'd been there. Some of the girls cried. Some were shocked. They didn't all understand it—but I don't think any of them'll ever forget it. It was the best graduation present you could have given the Senior Class. And me. [*She kisses him without shyness or apology.*] Thank you. [MERRILL *stands rigid, looking at* AGATHA.] I have to go now. They're all waiting for me. [*She starts to the door.*]

MERRILL. Ginny—

GINNY. [*Stops.*] Yes.

MERRILL. I'd like you to stay for a moment.

GINNY. The Seniors are starting to form—

MERRILL. This won't take long. Miss Reed and I have been discussing something I think you should know. [*He looks at* AGATHA.]

GINNY. Yes?

AGATHA. [*With great difficulty.*] Ginny— Yesterday I told you— [*She can't. She turns away.*]

MERRILL. If you won't tell her, I will.

GINNY. Tell me—what?

[AGATHA *is silent.*]

MERRILL. [*To* GINNY.] You kissed me just now. You haven't done that in a long time. I'm very grateful. But I can't accept it under false pretenses.

GINNY. False pretenses?

MERRILL. I had the movie shown—but not for the reasons you think. I did it because Miss Reed forced me to. Because she gave me an alternative that left me no choice. That's the truth and I want you to know it. [GINNY *just stands, looking at him.*] I don't want any more lies between us—there've been too many already. I can't wipe them out. But you're graduating today and the best present I can give you is a fresh start. I'm afraid I haven't been much of a father for quite a while. I'm sorry. [GINNY *turns her head to choke back the tears.* MERRILL *crosses to her.*] Ginny, I didn't tell you this to hurt you. I've never meant to hurt you—

GINNY. [*Turning to face him.*] You've forgotten a lot of things about me, haven't you? That I just don't cry when I'm sad.

That I cry just as much when I'm happy. [*Embracing him.*]
I don't care why you showed the picture. I never wanted you
to be a hero. I just wanted you to be honest. With me. And
with yourself.

ELLEN. [ELLEN *comes hurrying in. Breathless.*] Oh, there you
are, Jim. I've been all over—

AGATHA [*Pained at the interruption.*] Ellen, maybe you and
I could come back—

ELLEN. Well, not until I've had one moment with Jim. [*She
crosses to him.*] Now what is all this nonsense? Claude's terribly upset. I sneaked away and left him home on the telephone.
He's been on it all morning. First when he heard about the
movie—and then, right out of the blue—this *resignation*
thing—

AGATHA. Resignation?

[*As* GINNY *and* AGATHA *look at him,* MERRILL *moves away
from them to the window.*]

ELLEN. [*Crossing to* AGATHA.] I haven't seen Claude so worked
up since they had a strike in one of the plants.

AGATHA. When did this happen?

ELLEN. The letter came half an hour ago. [*To* MERRILL.] Oh,
I read it, Jim. It was lying on Claude's desk—and it was just
beautiful. Especially that part about self-respect. About your
feeling like a—what was it? It had something to do with eat-
ing—

AGATHA. An—educaterer?

ELLEN. That's it! Why, Ag, how clever of you!

AGATHA. [*Crossing to him.*] What happened, Jim?

MERRILL. [*Simply.*] I *did* see the picture. I stood in the back
of the theatre and watched them watching it. And I realized I
almost hadn't let them see it. That's when I knew everything

you said about me last night was true. That I had no right to be the President of this college—or any college.

ELLEN. [*Shocked.*] Ag, how could you say such a thing? I can't think of this college without Jim! And neither can the Board. You should hear them all arguing back there at home. About how much Jim's done for the school. And how it would look in the papers. And what a row the students would raise if they ever heard about it. Wouldn't they, Ginny?

GINNY. [*Happily.*] They'd raise a heck of a row!

ELLEN. Why, I'd even resign as Alumnae President!

[*Some* SENIORS, *going by the window to the Commencement parade, are chanting a class song. A voice calls, "Hey, Ginny! Did you forget? It's Commencement!"*]

GINNY. [*Shouting through the window.*] Okay—! [*Then.*] I've got to go now. [*She hurries to the door, then turns back for a moment.*] I always wondered why they called it Commencement. Now I know. [*She goes out.*]

ELLEN. I really have to go, too. I'm late already. But I just wanted to come and ask you to reconsider, Jim. [*Then, hesitantly.*] You won't mention this to Claude, will you? That I came over? He'll like thinking it was his own idea. It's kind of important for a man like Claude, you know. To think everything's his own idea.

MERRILL. [MERRILL *looks at her, then smiles.*] I'm afraid I've been underestimating you, Ellen.

ELLEN. You forgot, *I* was in your History class, too. I even got a B-plus.

MERRILL. A *B*.

ELLEN. Well, it's still the best mark I ever got. [*She smiles and exits.*]

[AGATHA *and* MERRILL *are left alone. There's a quiet moment.*]

AGATHA. I'm overwhelmed, Jim. I never expected all this.

MERRILL. We're even. Neither did I.

AGATHA. You know the trouble with most of us? We give up too easily. We forget that when you fight—you very often win. [*Then.*] *Will* you reconsider, Jim?

MERRILL. I don't know.

AGATHA. I think it's important to this college that you stay on.

MERRILL. I'm glad you do. But I want to be sure. [*Slowly.*] I've got a lot of thinking to do. A lot of catching up—

AGATHA. I've got a bit of catching up, myself. [*She sees a rose petal on the floor, picks it up, smiles in sudden appreciation.*]

MERRILL. Agatha— [*As she turns.*] When I came in here, it was because I wanted to tell you again that I was in love with you. That I didn't have much hope for it—after last night. But that somehow, today— [*He pauses, searching her face.*] I know we're different people than we were twenty years ago. I know a lot of things have changed. But I wouldn't want to kick myself for the rest of my life—for not trying. Do I have a chance?

AGATHA. [*After a moment.*] You might have had a hell of a chance, Jim. Except that I've had a standing offer for six years. And I think I'd better take it up before it runs out. If it hasn't run out already.

MERRILL. I see. [*Then.*] He's lucky. I wish I'd met you six years ago.

WOODY. [WOODY *enters. She stops short as she sees them in such close proximity. This is where she came in.*] Oh, I'm sorry. [*Backing up.*] I'll come back later.

MERRILL. It's all right, Miss Woods. I was just leaving. [*As he passes* WOODY, *she holds out her hand.*]

WOODY. I'd like to say— I think it's—

MERRILL. Thanks. [*Turning to* AGATHA.] See you in a few minutes?

AGATHA. I'll be there, Jim. [*He goes out.*]

WOODY. [WOODY *looks after him, sighing resignedly.*] Want to get into your cap and gown?

AGATHA. Yes.

[WOODY *starts toward the bedroom.* AGATHA *has been looking around the room with new eyes. Suddenly, she sees the sofa— laughs to herself.*]

WOODY. [*Turning at the bedroom door.*] What's the matter?

AGATHA. The sofa. It's so faded.

WOODY. Carted it all the way up from the basement. [*She exits.*]

AGATHA. [AGATHA *finishes her inspection of the room with real enjoyment. Suddenly she feels free—her mind begins to function at top speed. Briskly.*] What arrangements did you make for getting us out of here?

WOODY. [*Appearing like a shot in the door.*] Getting us— out—?

AGATHA. [AGATHA *takes her gown from the amazed* WOODY *and starts putting it on.*] We can drive into Boston and get the seven o'clock plane. Better call Wister tonight to set up that committee meeting in the morning. [WOODY *just stares at her.*] And call Senator Haines. Tell him he was right. I'll make a swing through the whole state before the election—get the Washington lead out of my pants. [*Enjoying it.*] Shut your mouth. You look like a fish.

WOODY. But, I thought—

AGATHA. That's your trouble. You think too much. You're so busy trying to figure things out ahead, you're always miles behind.

[COLE *enters. He looks angry and full of resolve.*]

COLE. I want to talk to you!

AGATHA. [*Seeing him for the first time.*] Not now—later.

COLE. Not later—now! [*To* WOODY.] Leave us alone. [*As she stands there.*] I said—leave us alone!

[WOODY *drops Agatha's cap on the sofa, and heads for the door. As she passes* COLE, *she gives him an approving nod. She doesn't know what the hell's going on, but she's for it. She shuts the door.*]

AGATHA. I thought you were on your way to bigger and better things.

COLE. You're not going to do it!

AGATHA. Do what?

COLE. You're the stubbornest dame I ever saw in my life. You're so goddam stubborn, you'd go ahead and *marry* him— [*With grim resolution.*] But you're not going to do it!

AGATHA. [*Enjoying it.*] Really?

COLE. Look, let's get one thing straight. I don't expect you to fall into my arms. I wouldn't even catch you if you did. One thing I found out this weekend. I *don't like women!*

AGATHA. [*If she could only laugh.*] Then why all the bother?

COLE. Because I'm neat! I straighten pictures— I put the tops on toothpaste tubes. I don't like leaving unfinished things around. You're not going to go through with this!

AGATHA. Aren't you being a little over-confident?

COLE. I don't think so. I'm offering you a deal. A business deal. [AGATHA's *smile fades.*] In exchange for such a small service, I'm giving you my personal guarantee that the *Life* article won't even hint at the colorful events leading up to your expulsion from this seat of higher learning. [AGATHA *takes an angry step toward him. He holds up his hand.*] See pictures on preceding page.

AGATHA. So you even eavesdrop!

COLE. Sure. [*With a smile.*] You learn all kinds of dirty tricks in *my* work, too.

[*There's a moment while* AGATHA *struggles between anger and appreciation. The latter wins, but* COLE *doesn't know it.*]

AGATHA [*Elaborately.*] Well, then it seems I have no choice. [*She crosses to the door, opens it, calls.*] Woody! [WOODY *enters almost immediately. She looks toward* COLE, *eagerly.*] Woody, there's been a change of plans. We'll drive into Boston and catch the seven o'clock plane. And call Wister tonight to set up that committee meeting in the morning. Oh yes—call Senator Haines and tell him I'll make a swing through the whole state before the election.

WOODY. [*Bewildered.*] But you just told me to—

AGATHA. I know. But there's been a *change of plans.* [AMELIA, MARY NELL, CLARISSE *and* JO *enter, all capped and gowned, and very excited.*]

AMELIA. We're your honor guard, Miss Reed!

AGATHA. I'm honored.

MARY NELL. Everything's on schedule. We're supposed to leave here as soon as the bells start to—

[*The college bells start peeling—all of them—all over campus, rich and mellow.*]

AMELIA. There they go.

AGATHA. [*Starting to the door.*] I'm ready.

CLARISSE. [*Hastily.*] Your cap—

AGATHA. [*Feeling her head.*] Oh, yes. [*She rushes back to the sofa and gets her cap, puts it on.*]

WOODY. Your speech! Where's your speech?

AGATHA. [*Hurrying to the desk.*] I left it on the desk. What did you do with it, Woody?

WOODY. [*Crossing behind her.*] It was there a minute ago.

[AGATHA *suddenly remembers. She stoops, fishes it triumphantly out of the wastebasket, as they* ALL *watch her.*]

AGATHA. [*Smoothing out the wrinkles.*] I found it! [*She starts to the door.*]

AMELIA. Got everything now?

AGATHA. [*As she passes* COLE, *a little smile.*] Everything.

[*She goes out, followed by the four* GIRLS. *There's a pause as* WOODY *looks after her, shaking her head.*]

WOODY. One weekend. [*Turning to* COLE.] A woman couldn't go crazy in one weekend, could she?

COLE. What's so crazy about changing her mind?

WOODY. Changing her mind? She told me the *same damned thing* five minutes ago!

COLE. [*Slowly.*] She—what?

WOODY. What do they put in the food around here? [*Comprehension sweeps over* COLE. *He reaches for* WOODY *and gives her a resounding kiss. She comes up for air.*] Now what's the matter with *you?*

COLE. Sweetheart, don't try to understand it. Just relax and enjoy it. [*He heads for the door like crazy as*

THE CURTAIN FALLS.]